D0870347

Practical Christianity

Practical Christianity

Divine Lessons for Daily Living
from the book of James

A.B. Simpson

CHRISTIAN PUBLICATIONS
CAMP HILL, PENNSYLVANIA

Christian Publications
3825 Hartzdale Drive, Camp Hill, PA 17011

Faithful, biblical publishing since 1883

ISBN: 0-87509-658-1
LOC: Catalog Card Number: 95-83826
© 1996 by Christian Publications, Inc.

96 97 98 99 00 5 4 3 2 1

Contents

1. The Practical Discipline of Life..............1

2. Practical Faith 15

3. Practical Obedience..............................29

4. Practical Love..45

5. The Practical Use of the Tongue 59

6. Practical Sanctification..........................75

7. The Practical Hope
   of the Lord's Coming 89

8. Practical Prayer....................................103

CHAPTER 1

The Practical Discipline of Life

> *Consider it pure joy, my brothers, whenever you face trials of many kinds. (James 1:2)*
> *Blessed is the man who perseveres under trial, because when he has stood the test, he will receive the crown of life that God has promised to those who love him. (1:12)*

Rotherham slightly changes the translation of these verses, as does also the Revised Version. "My brethren, count it all joy when we fall in with divers temptations" (1:2). "Blessed is the man that endureth temptation (or testings), for when he is *approved*, he shall receive the crown of life, which the Lord hath promised to them that love him" (1:12).

The epistles of Paul and John represent the interior, the experiential, and spiritual side of Christian life, while that of James represents the practical. God makes His mosaics of many different pieces and the blending of all together makes the perfect whole. There is room for James as well as for Paul and John. Paul is the apostle of faith, John of love,

1

Peter of comfort; but James is the apostle of good works, the apostle of practical living. He stands in the New Testament very much as the book of Proverbs stands in the Old. It has been said that the reason the Scotch are such a practical and prosperous race is because every Scotchman used to be brought up with the book of Proverbs in his vest pocket. It would be well to have some cheap editions of Proverbs and more pockets to hold them.

This conservative old minister in the church of Jerusalem, James, deals with the practical discipline of life from two sides.

The Discipline That Comes to Us Through Temptation

1. Not an Unmingled Evil

He first tells us that temptation is not an unmingled evil. By temptation he means undoubtedly evil; not trouble, but the solicitation of evil, the battle for right with the power of the tempter and our evil heart. "Consider it pure joy, my brothers, whenever you face trials [temptations, KJV] of many kinds" (1:2). "Blessed is the man who perseveres under trial [temptation, KJV]" (1:12). While it is evil, it has a good side, and it becomes an agency in the education of our spiritual character and the strengthening of all the better elements of our nature.

2. Overruled by God

While temptation is not directly from God, yet it is overruled by God, and made one of His instrumentalities of blessing to us. "God cannot be tempted by evil, nor does he tempt anyone" (1:13), yet God permits us to be tempted. God put our first parents into temptation and He made it possible for them either to choose or refuse; He gave them a nature subject to temptation, and while it might overcome them, it might also be overcome. God does not tempt any man, yet He does allow this to be one of the classes in the school of faith and holiness. He even led Jesus Christ, His own Son, into the wilderness by the Spirit to be tempted of the devil. Think it not a strange thing then, dear friends, if your life is called to pass through the ordeal of the conflict—evil from within and from without, not merely things that grieve, afflict and distress you, but things that tend to make you do wrong and draw you from the path of righteousness, truth and godliness. They will come. God wants you to be forewarned and forearmed, and to know it is better that they should come to you, if you but take the panoply of God and come through in victory.

3. The Source of Temptation

We should never forget where the source of temptation comes from. "Each one is tempted when, by his own evil desire, he is dragged away and enticed" (1:14). Temptation comes from your own heart. There are innumerable tempters: men, women and fallen spirits of wickedness. But none have any power unless we have ourselves a traitor in the citadel of the heart. The enemy cannot get in unless you let him in. You hold the key of the fortress. Therefore it is in your own heart that the crucial battle is fought, the secret foe is hidden—your own lust, your own desire or "coveting," which is the literal translation, the thing in you that wants to do the wrong, your wish for it, even if it is not yet your will. This is the starting place of temptation. It is that blossom of sin. And this is where God wants to bring His sanctifying grace and take away the very desire.

Just as the sea fowl plunging in the miry water comes up undefiled because its wing is oiled and burnished and the filth around cannot adhere to it, so the Lord Jesus passed through the powers of darkness and the allurements of the world and all the evil that was around Him and was proof against it. He could say "the prince of this world is coming. He has no hold on me" (John 14:30). It is in the heart that temptation has its starting point. Ask God to give you a true and holy desire to please Him, and an instinctive repugnance and recoil from evil; and so long as you have this, you shall not fall into temptation.

4. *The Blessedness of Resisting and Enduring Temptation*

Then we have the blessedness of resisting and enduring temptation. "Consider it pure joy, my brothers, whenever you face trials [temptations, KJV] of many kinds, because you know that the testing of your faith develops perseverance. Perseverance must finish its work so that you may be mature and complete, not lacking anything"

(James 1:2–4). "Blessed is the man who perseveres under trial [temptation, KJV]" (1:12). The battle does you good. The conflict educates you, strengthens you, establishes you, and is necessary for you that you may be grounded and settled and finally approved and rewarded. One of the best re-sults of temptation is that it shows you what is in your own heart. It reveals yourself. Until tempta-tion comes, you feel strong and self-confident; but when the keen edge of the adversary's weapon has pierced your soul, you have more sympathy with others and less confidence in your own self-suffi-ciency. You are humiliated and broken at His feet, a poor, helpless thing; and this is the best thing that can happen to you. God wants to disarm you and lay you low, and then He can lift and save you and give you His strength. It makes you hum-ble and doubtful of yourself. You find you must not take the aggressive, but fly to your refuge in Christ. "He will also provide a way out so that you can stand up under it" (1 Corinthians 10:13). Like the little conies that hide in the rock and do not face their enemies, but fly for shelter, you will find your only safeguard is Jesus Christ. He is the shield to cover you, and you will be safe not by fighting, but by hiding behind the cross and in the bosom of your Savior. If you have had much spiri-tual conflict, it has humbled you, shown you your helplessness, and taught you sympathy for others.

Temptation exercises our faith and teaches us to pray. It is like military drill and a taste of battle to the young soldier. It puts us under fire and compels us to exercise our weapons and prove their potency. It shows us the resources of Christ and the preciousness of the promises of God. It teaches us the reality of the Holy Spirit, and compels us to walk closely with Him and hide continually behind His strength and all-sufficiency. Every victory gives us new confidence in our victorious Leader, and new courage for the next onset of the foe, so that we become not only victors, but more than conquerors, taking the strength of our conquered foes and gathering precious spoil from each new battlefield. Temptation strengthens what we have received and establishes us in all our spiritual qualities and graces.

You will find the forest trees which stand apart, exposed to the double violence of the storm, are always the sturdiest and strike their roots the deepest in the soil. And so it is true in the spiritual world, as the Apostle Peter expressed it: "The God of all grace, who called you to his eternal glory in Christ, after you have suffered a little while, will himself restore you and make you strong, firm and steadfast" (1 Peter 5:10).

At the same time temptation teaches us to watch as well as pray, to avoid the things that bring temptation, and to keep off the enemy's ground. It is only the inexperienced Christian that plays lightly with evil. Luther used to say "He must needs have a long spoon who sups with the devil." "Pray," says Bishop Hamlin, "from God's side of the fence." Don't jump over into the devil's garden and then ask God to help you, but keep on God's side, and watch and pray that you enter not into temptation. Often our overconfidence betrays us. Like the man who had escaped the bailiff who tried to serve him with a warrant for arrest, and had just got across the state line, where the law protected him, when his pursuer, exchanging guile for force, laughed and said, "You have the best of me. And now let us shake hands and part friends." The foolish fellow reached out his hand, and in a moment the bailiff had pulled him over to his side of the line and clapped the handcuffs on him. So if Satan cannot beat us fairly, he will allure us so near the borders of danger that we will be caught by his wiles. Some people sail so near the lake of fire that they get their sails scorched and find it impossible to get away. The maturest Christian is always the humblest and most watchful. Let us be not high-minded, but fear, and learn to combine the two blessed safeguards of hope and fear, which God has so wisely blended in these two passages: "So, if you think you are standing firm, be careful that you don't fall!" (1 Corinthians 10:12), and then in the 13th verse, "God is faithful; he will not let you be tempted beyond what you can bear." And yet once more, in the 14th verse, he returns to the language of warning and caution, "Therefore, my dear friends, flee from idolatry."

Temptation also teaches us patience. "Perseverance must finish its work so that you may be mature and complete, not lacking anything"

(James 1:4). This implies that patience is the finishing grace of the Christian life. Therefore, God usually puts His children through the school of suffering last. It is the graduation class in the discipline of Christ. Let us not, therefore, be surprised if God puts us through the hottest of all furnaces, namely, that which is fired with the devil's brimstone, before He makes us vessels for His glory.

5. Temptation Brings a Reward

Temptation brings a glorious recompense of reward, for "because when he has stood the test, he will receive the crown of life that God has promised to those who love him" (1:12). There is a reward for the soul-winner. There is a reward for the Christian pastor and worker. But there is also a special reward for the man or the woman who has had no great service, and perhaps has won no single soul, but who has stood in the hard place, has kept sweet in the midst of wrong, and in the face of temptation, pure amid the allurements of the world, and simply withstood in the evil day, and having done all, stood at last approved.

On the field of Waterloo, there was a regiment which stood under fire through all that awful day and was not once suffered to charge upon the enemy. It held the key to the position, and as again and again permission to advance was asked, the answer came, "Stand firm." When they had nearly all fallen, the message came back for the last time from their commander, "You have saved the day," and the answer was returned, "You will find us all here." Sure enough they lay a heap of slain on that fatal, yet glorious hill. They had simply stood, and history has given them the reward of valor and the imperishable fame of having turned the tide of the greatest battle of the 19th century. So God is preparing crowns for quiet lives, for suffering women, for martyred children, for the victims of oppression and wrong, for the silent sufferers and the lonely victors who just endured temptation. Tempted brother, be of good cheer. Some day you will wonder at the brightness of your crown.

God's Providence and Our Discipline

In the striking parable of the potter and the wheel, Jeremiah has taught us that while God is disciplining the heart by the touch of His Spirit, He is turning round the clay on the wheel of providence and bringing us into new situations for the exercise of new graces and the teaching of new lessons with every alteration of life's conditions. So His providence cooperates with His Holy Spirit in the education of our spiritual character, and we are to recognize the things that happen to us as in no sense accidents, but simply divine methods of dealing with us and teaching and blessing us. So James proceeds to bring out the relation of God's providence to our spiritual discipline: "The brother in humble circumstances ought to take pride in his high position. But the one who is rich should take pride in his low position" (1:9–10).

1. The Discipline of Prosperity

We have the discipline of prosperity. This is not a hard or uncongenial experience to the natural heart, but it often is the hardest of all experiences for the soul. "I have learned," says Paul, "to be content whatever the circumstances. I know what it is to be in need, and I know what it is to have plenty [abound, KJV]" (Philippians 4:11–12). But how few Christians really know how to abound. How frequently prosperity changes their temper and the habits and fruits of their lives! To receive God's blessing in temporal things, to have wealth suddenly thrust upon us, to be surrounded with the congenial friends, to be enriched with all the happiness that love, home, the world's applause and unbounded prosperity can give, and yet to keep a humble heart, to be separated from the world in its spirit and in its pleasures, to keep our hearts in holy indifference from the love and need of earthly things, to stand for God as holy witnesses in the most public station, and to use our prosperity and wealth as a sacred trust for Him, counting nothing our own, and still depending upon Him as simply as in the days of penury—this, indeed, is an experience rarely found, and only possible through the infinite grace of God. And yet God calls His children in greater or less measure to pass through the test of blessing.

It may not be a great fortune, but a joy in your humble life worth more to you than millions. Now He does not ask us to refuse it, to be harsh, narrow and monkish, and think to make ourselves better by asperities and penances. No, "The brother in humble circumstances ought to take pride in his high position" (James 1:9). Open your heart to the love and joy He is bringing. Bask in the sunshine of His smile. But do it with a humble and unselfish heart. Let your blessing only make you more sensitive to the sufferings of others, more grateful to Him, and more ready to make sacrifices and render services to your Master and your fellow men. Then can God rejoice over you to do you good with all His heart and with all His soul.

2. The Discipline of Adversity

Then comes the other side of the revolving wheel, the discipline of adversity. The brother of high degree is made low. Wealth takes wings and flies away. Friends prove false, and even the downy nest of love and home breeds viper's eggs and bitter heartbreaks. But we must still rejoice. God is testing us in the crucible. We have a witness for Him that only the dark shadows can bring out. Let us be true to our testimony. Let us glorify Him in the fires. Let us look over the head of all our trouble to Him, and still believe that "in all things God works for the good of those who love him" (Romans 8:28). Then nothing can be against us.

And sorrow touched by God grows bright
  With more than rapture's ray,
As darkness shows us worlds of light
  We never saw by day.

Adversity often has to come to save us from the loss of eternal life. Then only when all other things fail us, can we fully find the all-sufficiency of God, and learn that within ourselves we may possess the resources of perfect happiness by having Him. It was thus that the Hebrew Christians could take joyfully the spoiling of their goods, knowing in themselves that they had a better and more enduring substance (Hebrews 10:34).

It is a rare secret in the alchemy of grace to be able thus to transmute a seeming flaw into an eternal touch of grace and glory.

A lapidary once purchased a beautiful stone, but found afterwards that there was a hidden flaw of iron rust beneath the surface. At first he was disposed to throw it away as worthless. Then there came to him the conception of a rich design, in which a female figure was cut in the stone, and the strong tint of the iron vein was carved into a rich robe whose drapery and color added a beautiful adorning to the exquisite figure. Thus the flaw became the fairest charm in all the fine creation of his genius. And so God would have us take the things that seem to be against us and so transmute them by the power of His grace that "instead of the thornbush will grow the pine tree,/ and instead of briers the myrtle will grow" (Isaiah 55:13).

In conclusion let us learn to find in God the secret of blessing and victory under all conditions and circumstances, and even to turn the hate of Satan into an occasion of victory and blessing. Thus shall the curse be made a blessing, sorrow turned into joy, and even sin so conquered that grace shall much more abound.

CHAPTER 2

Practical Faith

*If any of you lacks wisdom, he should ask God,
who gives generously to all without finding fault,
and it will be given to him. But when he asks, he
must believe and not doubt, because he who doubts
is like a wave of the sea, blown and tossed by the
wind. That man should not think he will receive
anything from the Lord. (James 1:5–7)*

There is nothing in the world more practical than
faith. It may seem to the naturalist a very
dreamy, speculative thing, but when we stop to
think, we will readily see that the most practical
thing in life is confidence. Like the law of gravitation
which holds the universe together, the principle of
cohesion that binds human society is confidence between man and man. Take it away from the home,
and where would the family be? Take it away from
business, and where would your bank and stock ex-
changes be? Take it away from the State, and we
have revolution, anarchy, socialism and the uproot-
ing of the foundations of society.

A few months ago a certain stock went up from 16 points to 160 points. When the manipulation was sufficient to make several millionaires, then confidence failed. We were told in the newspapers of yesterday that 50 million dollars were waiting for a certain financial scheme. The moment a franchise was secured, a mighty structure would be spanned across the Hudson River, and all our complicated lines of transportation directly connected with New York. The money is ready for this, but all that is necessary is confidence. If confidence is a fortune in business, how much more in the higher realm?

The scientist believes, and risks everything for his beliefs. The Prince of Wales was standing beside Professor Playfair once, near a cauldron of boiling lead at white heat. The professor said: "I am going to ask you to put your hand in that cauldron and ladle out a handful of that lead." "Do you tell me to do it?" asked the Prince. "Yes, but wait a moment." He then washed the Prince's hand with ammonia that there might be no oil on his flesh. The Prince put his hand in the cauldron and poured out some of the boiling lead without injury. He believed the word of the scientist and risked his life upon it, just because he had confidence.

We owe this continent to the fact that a humble Italian believed in a great West—to him a great East—and he plodded on in his faith. He met rebuffs and refusals, but his vessels were at last launched, and Christopher Columbus discovered America, because he believed in it.

Palissy worked a long time to develop the secrets of his exquisite art. His wife reviled him, and his children pleaded with him to give up his foolishness and settle down to honest work. He saw only this mighty secret, he believed in it and he worked it out; his faith became a fact and in consequence was crowned with triumph and success.

So it is that everything that is of value in the world has come from the confidence of some great soul who pressed on till triumph was achieved and his efforts were crowned with success.

And so in the higher world, the mightiest force is faith. It is the law of Christianity. Paul calls it the "law of faith" (Romans 3:27, KJV). It is just as mighty a law in the spiritual world as gravitation is in the material world. It binds us to God, and then to one another. So Abraham goes out, leaving the culture and wealth of that ancient civilization, out into the wilderness, an emigrant, and God gives him a new kingdom, and all our hopes have sprung from that old pioneer believer who dared to risk everything upon God.

Thus Joseph goes down and down for years, until his life is crushed and "the iron enters his soul." But he believes through it all in the vision of his youth, and he comes up again, as every true believer does at last, and becomes the lord of Egypt, and transforms the destiny of two nations.

We find the Old and the New Testament full of the triumphs of faith, until at last Jesus Himself becomes the "Prince Leader" of our faith, and achieves His miracles and works His mighty deeds by faith in God. When asked why the fig tree withered, He said faith had caused it. At the grave of Lazarus he said, "Father, I thank you that you have heard me. I knew that you always hear me" (John 11:41–42). It was faith. He never doubted God. He always expected the thing to come to pass that He claimed.

So He has left to us the secret. Paul has told us we may "have the faith of the Son of God" (Galatians 2:20, KJV), the very same touch that He had; we may link with Omnipotence just as He did. There are just two things that are almighty, God and faith. The man that believes God just comes into partnership with God and shares His all-sufficiency. We know that in the natural world the mightiest forces are those we do not see—not the mountains, but the principle that holds them together; not the worlds, but the law that moves them; not the things we touch, but the hidden forces that control them. And we are being taught by the progress of our age to believe in nature's forces and to use them as levers to lift our loads and as motors to move our engines. So in the spiritual world faith is the power to attach ourselves to God.

There are two ways to do things—faith and works; one to do them yourself, the other to let God do them. The power of faith is not how much can I do, but how much can God do? Faith saves us just because it puts us into God's hands. It drops us into the salvation that He has already finished, and we have only to accept. Faith sancti-

fies us, not because it would have us do better, but
it brings the power to do it. So faith heals, not by
slowly building up the tissues and blood, but by
putting a new electric fountain of vitality in your
frame that makes an old man young, and although
ready to drop into the grave keeps you by a second life. Faith brings the answers to your prayers,
because it takes God's prayers instead of yours,
and then they must be answered, because they are
His asking, claiming and commanding. Faith puts
us out and brings God in, and our life becomes a
supernatural one. Faith is, therefore, a practical
force, the secret of all real power, and a secret
which can be applied to everything in our life. Let
us now examine the exposition of faith as we find
it in the Epistle of James.

The Principle of Faith

We are taught the principle of faith—what it is
and how it comes.

It must be absolute and unwavering. You cannot have a half faith. It must be not doubting. The
element of uncertainty destroys the vitality of
faith just as much as a scratch defaces a mirror,
and as a little chip in the side of your grain of corn
kills the germ. The faith which accomplishes om-
nipotent results is confidence, boldness and the
full assurance of faith.

Next we are told that faith is the receiving or-
gan of the soul, that without it we cannot receive
anything of the Lord. "God . . . gives generously
to all without finding fault" (James 1:5), or "of

course," as Alford translates it. God always gives. But the unbelieving heart cannot receive. It is fettered and paralyzed by its doubts, and like the sensitive plant shrinks helplessly, and misses the blessing that His love would gladly have bestowed. "That man should not think he will receive anything from the Lord" (1:7).

Faith and Wisdom

"If any of you lacks wisdom, he should ask God. . . . But when he asks, he must believe and not doubt" (1:5–6). Wisdom is that quality which enables us to suit the right means to the end in view. It is wholly practical and concerned not with theories and ideas, but with actual conditions and the way to meet them. It teaches us how to live, and enables us to meet every emergency rightly and successfully. It does not mean that we are infallible. It is not the wisdom of our common sense and level-headedness. It presupposes our ignorance and fallibility, and takes God's wisdom instead of our own. Even when we cannot understand His leading, faith still can trust Him that it will be right in the end. Even when we err, God's wisdom can still overrule our mistake and bring blessing out of it in the end.

Spurgeon used to tell about a weather vane which had the text inscribed above it, "God is love." When he asked the old miller why he put the verse on top of it, he said that it might speak to the people at all points of the compass and say to them, "God is love, whichever way the wind blows." So faith in God's wisdom counts upon His goodness and faithfulness in the face of all conditions and in spite of all hindrances.

John Vassar used to say that he doubted whether our so-called mistakes were mistakes always. Knocking at a door one day in quest of a woman with whom he wished to speak about her soul, a different person met him, and told him that he had made a mistake, and that she did not live there. The good man answered, "I guess it is not a mistake after all, but the Lord wants me to talk to you instead." And so tactfully breaking through the barrier of her strangeness, he reached her heart, and ended by leading her to the Savior.

I recall an incident in the early history of this work through which I was strangely led to lease as my residence for a year the dwelling in which all the Alliance work began in this city. I had been offered the house by a friend who owned it, and after much prayer had decided that it was the Master's will that I should take it. But on almost the last day of the season I was informed that the house had just been sold to a neighbor who was determined to live in it himself. All efforts to induce this man to consent to my occupying the house were vain, and the only thing left was to accept the house that the man was leaving instead, as the season was late, and moving day came within 24 hours. Against every inclination I became convinced that it was the Lord's will for me to consent to this arrangement. After a great struggle I called to sign the lease for the unwelcome house, which was most unattractive in every way. To my surprise, however, the gentleman came out to greet me, and immediately explained that he had changed his mind and decided to stay where he was, and that he would be glad to lease the other house that he had just purchased, as we desired. The strange reason of it all was that that very day he had attended the funeral of an old friend in the country, and that he and his wife had come home with the feeling that if they moved something might happen to them. It was a mere superstition, but God had allowed it to come in order to change his mind and accomplish the purpose to which He had been leading all the time.

There is nothing in the whole circle of our commonplace life that we may not bring to God in faith, and thus find a hundred Ebenezers every day all along the path of life.

Faith and Works

In the second chapter of James the apostle takes up the practical side of faith, and shows that it is not idle dreaming, but stepping out and acting according to our convictions. There are works that are not the works of faith, but the works of fear, doubt and human dependence. But there are works which must follow faith, if it is genuine and vital. When the nobleman believed the word that Jesus had spoken for the healing of his boy, he was bound to stop his praying, and go back to meet the answer that had been promised. When the cripple at Lystra

believed the gospel which Paul preached, immediately he rose up and leaped and walked. "If I
believed," said an infidel, "as you say you do,
that the world was perishing and that Christ
alone could save it, I would abandon every interest and fly to the ends of the earth to tell men
the story of salvation." As poor crippled Tom
used to say, "Knowin' is lovin' and lovin' is
doin'; and if we're not a doin' on it, we don't
love Him, that's all."

Faith and Healing

"And the prayer offered in faith will make the
sick person well; the Lord will raise him up"
(5:15). Surely this is practical faith, a faith that
comes down to the level of our daily life and all
our physical needs. This was the sort of faith that
James believed in. And was he not right? If God
cannot help us in the things we see, how can we
expect Him to help us in the world of the future
and the unseen?

In these days of materialism and unbelief on
one hand, and fanaticism on the other; when the
supernatural and scriptural conceptions of divine
healing are in danger of being confounded with
the vagaries of Christian Science and the ex-
travagances of modern "apostles" and faith heal-
ers, it is more important than ever that a sober
and conservative, yet bold and uncompromising
testimony be given to the true doctrine of the
Lord's healing. While this truth has not the first
place in our testimony, it has a very important

place; and the experience which it has brought us has become a turning point in the life and work of multitudes whom God has used in the teaching of deeper truth and the work of missions. While we do not go forth to be the special apostles of divine healing, yet we owe much of our ministry on the higher and more spiritual planes to this truth and its blessed influence.

It is most distinctly promised here to the prayer of faith. What the prayer of faith is the Apostle James has already told us in the first chapter. It is the prayer of the man who believes, nothing wavering, that he receives the things he asks. It involves three steps. First, to believe that divine healing is provided for us in the Word of God and in the work of Christ. Second, to come to God and actually claim it for ourselves by a definite act of committal. And third, to act as if we had it, and step out and prove our faith by our works.

Over in Flamborough, Ontario, there lives a young farmer named Patterson, whose parents are well known to me, and whose brother is one of our most prominent official workers. A few years ago he broke his leg, and the village doctor came and set it, showing the family beforehand how serious the compound fracture was, so that the father told afterwards how he had with his own hand felt the great void between the broken bones. The limb was tied with splints as usual and stretched out in a horizontal position, and the patient told to keep in that position for several weeks. Next morning to the surprise of the family, young Patterson was out feeding the cattle at the usual hour and doing his work as if nothing had happened. The explanation was this: During the night the Lord had spoken to him something on this wise, "Have I not healed you often before, and can't you trust Me now? Then, if you trust Me what are you going to do about it?" The young man knew the Lord and had proved Him. And so he quietly got up, took off the splints, and lay down again until daylight, and then arose and dressed himself and went about his work, and has been going about it ever since. That is the prayer of faith.

Faith and Service

Higher than healing, infinitely more important than helping people out of their troubles, is the climax to which James conducts us in the closing verses, after having told us that "The prayer of a righteous man is powerful and effective" (5:16). Here is faith's highest triumph and its noblest ministry. "My brothers, if one of you should wander from the truth and someone should bring him back, remember this: Whoever turns a sinner from the error of his way will save him from death and cover over a multitude of sins" (5:19–20). How is this to be accomplished? It is given to the ministry of faith, the faith that works by love. How will your children be saved? "Believe in the Lord Jesus, and you will be saved—*you and your household*" (Acts 16:31, italics added). Read the story of Jerry McAuley and you will find that after his conversion, he often "erred from the truth" and had to be re-converted, or, rather, brought back to the fold; and but for the patient, untiring love of a humble missionary, who used to pursue him, when he tried to slip out of the meeting unobserved, and hold him back from the river thieves, and was always saying to him, "Jerry, keep on trying, keep on trying, and it will be all right at last"—but for this, the story of his wondrous life and his harvest of precious souls would never have been told.

In a wretched attic in London there lived a lad named Tom Reed, a poor cripple, who was sometimes able to drag himself to the corner and sweep the street crossing for a penny, and sometimes even to find his way to the little mission round the corner, where they told about Jesus and His love. His only earthly friends were his grandmother, who gave him a scant living, and Jack Lee, his pal. One day Jack called to say good-bye, as he started to the country for a new field of operations in his humble trade. And he brought Tom a shilling as his parting gift, telling him that he must use it for something he "wanted partikler." Then Tom told him that what he wanted "most partikler" was a Bible. Jack tried to laugh him out of it, for "these here books," he said, were only for scholars, and not for such as they. But Tom begged hard, and at last Jack went out and got the Bible, adding as he left him that the bookseller had told him that the book was all right and might make his fortune yet. It wasn't long till Tom had devoured it, and was so full of it that he felt he must do something for

his Savior and his fellow sinners. So he denied
himself his daily mug of milk to buy some paper
and a pencil, and began to write verses of his Bible
on bits of paper. After praying over them and wa-
tering them with his tears, he would address the
outside, "Passerby, please read," and drop them
out of the window. One day a handsome gentleman climbed the rickety stairs and asked if he was
the boy who dropped the papers out of the window. And then he told Tom with much feeling
that he had come to thank him for the blessing he
had brought him, and how his own son in the
country, a suffering and dying boy, had pleaded
with him to find some service to do for God, so
that he would not go empty-handed to meet his
Master. The verse that he had picked up was this:
"I must work the works of him that sent me, while
it is day" (John 9:4, KJV), and it had changed his
whole purpose and life. Tom did not want any
thanks. "I only do the writin'," he said, "He does
the blessin'." But the gentleman undertook the
care of Tom henceforth in his little attic, and went
to live out his lesson. He built a mission chapel for
his boy, and souls were saved, and Tom's warning
message to him was faithfully lived out. "Tell
your rich friends that if they are not workin' for
Him they don't know Him, for workin' is lovin',
and lovin' is doin'." One day there came a little
parcel to the mission. It was Tom's old Bible, un-
derlined and stained with many a tear, for Tom
had gone above, where "their deeds will follow
them" (Revelation 14:13). And for many a day the

old Bible continued to live out its owner's life, and "he still speaks, even though he is dead" (Hebrews 11:4). God give us the faith that knows and loves and does for Jesus' sake. Amen.

CHAPTER 3

Practical Obedience

Do not merely listen to the word, and so deceive yourselves. Do what it says. Anyone who listens to the word but does not do what it says is like a man who looks at his face in a mirror and, after looking at himself, goes away and immediately forgets what he looks like. But the man who looks intently into the perfect law that gives freedom, and continues to do this, not forgetting what he has heard, but doing it—he will be blessed in what he does. (James 1:22–25)

Practical obedience naturally follows the subject of practical faith. Trust and obey are the two wings which maintain the equilibrium of our flight, the two oars which keep us steadily in the channel of our course. This paragraph unfolds some of the profoundest ethical principles of the New Testament.

The Will of God

First, there is the will of God as the supreme authority of right and duty.

"The Father of the heavenly lights, who does not change like shifting shadows. He chose [of his own will, KJV] to give to us birth through the word of truth" (James 1:17–18). Here our very conversion is referred back to the will of God as its supreme source. And God Himself is recognized as the Sovereign Being who sits enthroned in His eternal, unchangeable and infallible authority and righteousness as the Sovereign of our being and of all being. The figure here involved in the beautiful original phrase is that of the parallax by which the astronomer measures the distance of the remotest stars. The parallax is the angle formed by two points on the earth's surface from which an observation is taken of a distant star according to the angle made. From these two points we measure the distance of the star by the acuteness of the angle. But with God, James says there is no parallax. Looking at Him from every standpoint He is eternally the same and His will is forever the same. Therefore, there is a fixed standard of right and wrong, and duty is not a mere accommodation to circumstances, sentiments or human opinions, but conformity to the will of God.

The Word of God

This passage presents the Word of God as the standard of right and wrong. For this supreme Lawgiver has given us a law, and has revealed to us His will concerning our conduct. That law is here called "the perfect law that gives freedom" (1:25). It is a perfect law. There is no greater mir-

acle in the Bible than its revelation of righteousness. Even the Decalogue itself, although not
nearly so perfect in its primal edition at Sinai as it
has become through the teachings of the Son of
Man, and as reissued and reenacted by Him
through the Sermon on the Mount and His wise
and holy teachings, is a marvelous monument of
the wisdom and righteousness of God. One of our
American Justices, it is said, was converted from
infidelity to Christianity by studying the Mosaic
Law. "Where did Moses get that Law?" he asked
himself after carefully reading and analyzing it.
There is nothing in the literature of Egypt, Chal-
dea or Greece from which he could have derived
its profound and comprehensive principles of ju-
risprudence. Everything is there in the most con-
densed and comprehensive form. Under two great
tables he classifies our duty to God and to one another, and covers all ethical questions with sublime simplicity and completeness. He must have
got it from heaven. And so he did. And as we read
it in its larger edition in the spiritual teachings of
the New Testament, it claims the subjection of
our conscience, the homage of our will, the obedience of our life, and we are constrained to say of
it, as Jehovah said of His ancient commandments,
that it is "for our good always" (Deuteronomy
6:24, KJV).

The Law of Liberty

Here in James it is described by a new phrase,
"the perfect law of liberty" (James 1:25, KJV).

This is the New Testament law, the law of love. As it came to us from Sinai, it was not the law of liberty, but of condemnation. But now with its penalty met in the person of Christ, and its motive power supplied by His Holy Spirit and His indwelling life in our heart, it becomes to us not the authority of necessity, but the constraint of love. It is the law in our heart becoming part of our nature so that we keep it, not because we have to, but because we love to. As citizens of the State we do not avoid the crime of murder because we fear that we will be electrocuted if we murder, but because our nature lifts us above it. We do not want to murder. We are under the law of liberty. We make the law ourselves, and so long as we keep it, we are free from it, for the "law is made not for the righteous but for lawbreakers and rebels" (1 Timothy 1:9). The obedient are lifted above it, and are free from its condemnation and its bondage.

The Grafted Word

A new figure is here introduced (James 1:21, KJV). The principle of grafting is very simple and suggestive. On a common root or stock a cultivated bud or branch is fastened and trained to grow into its new trunk and stem until all its vegetable organism has become connected with the new fountainhead. And then it begins to bear, not the fruit of the old stem, which is but a common crab or wild vine, but the cultivated fruit in all its mellowness and delicacy of flavor. It is really drawing upon the life of the old root, but crowning it with new beauty and richest fruitfulness. So upon the stem of our natural life God engrafts His Word, and so infuses and inworks that Word into our very life that it becomes the element of our being and the second nature of all our habits, controlling us without arbitrary constraint and making it our delight to do His will. Thus it becomes to us a law of liberty. We do right because we want to. We serve God because we love Him. Obedience becomes as natural as sin was before, and the heart is spontaneous and free in all its spiritual affections and actions. Obedience, therefore, is not a matter of outward authority, but inward impulse. Character is not built as you would build a house, by adding plank and timber to timber from the outside, but as God builds a tree, by throwing out life from the inside, and adding each new layer from the heart out.

This is the secret of liberty and power in all the natural and spiritual world. Take the laws of the physical realm and get them incorporated into your industrial art, and what power they exercise! Take the law of electricity and put it in your house as a telephone, and it will carry your messages for hundreds of miles. Put it in your towns and cities as a telegraph system, and it will traverse continents and oceans with its messages of fire. Put it in your vehicles, and it will carry your trolleys and your automobiles. Put it in your factories, and it will become the motive power of all business, transportation and commerce. But let it get beyond your control, disobey it, and it will strike you lifeless with the lightning's awful blaze. So the Word of God must be received, incorporated, engrafted and assimilated into our spiritual being, and then it becomes the motive power of our being and the guide of our life.

The Moral Conditions

The passage presents the moral conditions which hinder the free operation of the Word of God in our lives.

"Therefore, get rid of all moral filth and the evil that is so prevalent and humbly accept the word planted in you, which can save you" (1:21). Just as the electric current must be insulated before it can be operated, so the Word of God cannot work freely in a soul that willingly indulges in sin. Two forms of evil are here classified, one the impure, the other the malignant. Filthiness includes all forms of sensual indulgence; naughtiness all forms of bitter and malicious feeling. Either of these will cloud the spiritual vision and interrupt the life of God in the heart. Just as the compass on shipboard can be deflected from its true direction by a counter-attraction through some piece of metal thoughtlessly left on deck, so conscience, though sincere, may be warped and misdirected by the influence of unholy desire of indulgence, and the soul perverted even when flattering itself that it is acting with the deepest sincerity and doing that which it believes to be right. There must, therefore, be a spirit of surrendered self-will and holy meekness, if we would receive the engrafted word. The Apostle Peter expresses the same truth in almost identical terms, "Therefore, rid yourselves of all malice and all deceit, hypocrisy, envy, and slander of every kind. Like newborn babies, crave pure spiritual milk, so that by it you may grow up in your salvation" (1 Peter 2:1–2). Therefore it has come to pass that this same Word of God has been used to defend the most unholy teachings by men whose judgment was biased by a wrong heart, and whose conscience was perverted by an unsanctified spirit.

The Self-Revealing Poser

James talks about the self-revealing power of the Word of God. It is here compared to a mirror, and the ordinary hearer of the Word to a man beholding his natural face in the glass. But the hasty glance passes, and he "immediately forgets what he looks like" (James 1:24). The true hearer is represented by the man who takes a nearer view of himself in the sacred mirror, and becomes not a forgetful hearer of the Word, but a doer. Literally translated, this should read, "But the man who looks intently into the perfect law that gives freedom, and continues to do this, not forgetting what he has heard, but doing it—he will be blessed in what he does" (1:25). The beginning of all self-improvement is self-knowledge, and the most wholesome knowledge we can have of ourselves is to know our faults. "Blessed are the poor in spirit,/ for theirs is the kingdom of heaven" (Matthew

5:3). Blessed are they that are dissatisfied, for they shall be satisfied, so this has been happily translated. It is thus that the Word of God sanctifies us by showing us first our need, and then leading us to Christ for the supply. We look into the picture of love first in the 13th chapter of First Corinthians, and we see how little we have of the love that "is patient [and] is kind" (13:4). Humbled by a sense of our failure, we take Christ for the grace of love. We bring our strifes and quarrels to the teaching of Jesus in the 18th and 19th chapters of Matthew, and we begin to settle our disputes according to the Word.

Thus we "discern ourselves," and by true self-judgment we escape the divine judgment and rise to a higher righteousness, taking Christ as our sanctification over against our self-condemnation. The willingness to see ourselves in our true light is the very highest proof of a true heart. "The fear of the LORD is the beginning of wisdom" (Proverbs 9:10). And the best evidence that there is no hidden sin covered up in our heart is our readiness to say, "Search me, O God, and know my heart;/ test me and know my anxious thoughts./ See if there is any offensive way in me,/ and lead me in the way everlasting" (Psalm 139:23–24).

The Blessedness of Doing

"He will be blessed in what he does" (James 1:25). Having seen our fault and also the vision of God's highest will for us, now follows the responsibility of practical obedience. James is a thorough believer in good works. He is no musty ascetic living in pensive cloisters and dreaming his life away in self-centered introspection, but a man of wholesome action carrying his religion into the light of day and the field of human life and helpful duty. It is in the doing that the blessing comes.

1. The Secret of Faith

This is the remedy for doubt and the secret of faith. "If anyone chooses to do God's will, he will find out whether my teaching comes from God or whether I speak on my own" (John 7:17). Don't argue with your skeptic. Say to him as Christ used to say, "Come and see." Prove Christianity by testing it. Go to God with even the little faith you have, or if you have nothing but doubt to bring, go with your doubt. Tell Him the worst. If you can only pray, "O God, if there be a God, help me," He will hear that cry.

I once knew of an intelligent infidel being converted by what might be called an unconscious prayer. His Christian wife had just died, and in the remembrance of her beautiful life and still more beautiful death, his heart was bursting with agony. Before he realized it, he had uttered a sob of prayer to her God for comfort and help. Instantly he remembered that he did not believe in her God; but before he had time to recall his prayer by an act of reasoning, it had reached heaven through an impulse of his heart, and the answer had come back to him in a new consciousness such as he had never felt before. From that moment he knew there was a God. He had proved Him by the practical test.

2. *The Way to Find Salvation*

This is the best way to find salvation. Take it as Christ has freely offered it, and then begin to act as if you had it, and you will be blessed in your doing. The best formula for beginning a Christian life that we have ever heard is the simple resolution of Hendly Vivars the night in which he turned away from a life of ungodliness to follow Christ, "If this be true for me, I will live from this moment as a man that has been cleansed from all sin by the blood of Christ." That decision put him on salvation ground, and from that moment he was a Christian. The most happy and useful Christian I have ever known was a gentleman who struggled for months for a religious experience without any result, and then quietly walked into the woods one day and made this resolution, "From this moment I will serve Christ as my Master whether I am lost or saved. My business is to follow Him. The responsibility of my salvation rests with Him." Before 24 hours had passed, that man was rejoicing in the experience that he had stopped seeking, and was blessed in his doing.

3. *Realizing the Experience and the Baptism*

This is the way to realize the experience of Christ's indwelling and the baptism of the Spirit. Simply yield yourself to God and claim the promise of the Spirit. And then begin to act as if you had Him as your Sanctifier, Keeper and indwelling Life, and He will answer to your expectation and meet your faith. If you venture on Him, He will be there every time. It is the doing that brings the blessing.

4. The Action in Healing

Are you seeking for healing? Christ never healed anybody on his back or his bed. "Stretch out your hand" (Matthew 12:13), was His prescription to the man with the withered hand. "Get up! Pick up your mat and walk" (John 5:8), was His command to the paralytic. "Go, show yourselves to the priests" (Luke 17:14), He said to the lepers, and "as they went they were cleansed" (17:14). "You may go. Your son will live" (John 4:50), He told the anxious father, and as he was obeying, the message met him that the healing had come. It was in doing something they all received the blessing. And so still we must show our faith by our works, and find strength in stepping out even in our weakness, and throwing ourselves upon the strength of God for life's duties and demands.

5. The Key to Finding Happiness

Would you find joy and happiness? Again it will meet you in doing the will of God. "Well done, good and faithful servant!" (Matthew 25:21), is the significant benediction of the Master, "come and share your master's happiness!" (25:21). It is duty well done that brings the joy of the Lord.

"What is heaven?" said one of our eccentric preachers. "I'll tell you what heaven is. It's out yonder in that little back street where a poor widow is weeping over her roofless children and sitting on her boxes and furniture on the street. Go to her with a basket of groceries, a load of coal and a good-sized bank note for her unpaid rent, and you will soon find what heaven is." And the hard-fisted hearer came next day to tell Mr. Jones that he had been in heaven the last 24 hours, ever since he had found that poor widow and helped her out of her distress.

I remember a New Year long ago in my own experience when I dedicated a whole month, beginning with the week of prayer, to wait in my musty old study for a fuller baptism of the Spirit. I had received the Spirit, but I was straining after something more. Day after day I prayed, and left my duties largely undone. Thicker grew the murky air, and darker the visions of my troubled brain. More intense became my sensations and temptations, and more terrible the struggle with my feelings and my spiritual foes. But still I persevered, expecting surely some mighty blessing. At last one day when my brain was almost bursting with the strain, I turned to my Bible with a cry for direction and help. Before me in letters of light I read, "He is not here, He is risen. He goeth before you into Galilee. There shall ye see Him. Go ye and teach all nations" (see Matthew 28, KJV). In a moment the message was plain. Not dreaming, but doing. And as I went forth from that cloister to the bedsides of the sick and the pressing duties of a sad world, lo, the light returned, the sky cleared, the Master was revealed, the Lord drew nigh, and a blessing came which has never ceased through all these years to meet me still, as I go forth in self-forgetting love to bless others, to pray for others and to find the fellowship of the Master in doing His perfect will.

6. *The Things That Count the Most*

Finally, in the work of the Lord and the ministry of our Christian service we shall find that what we do and what we are count for more than what we say. Missionary Richards preached for many years with little effect to the savages of the Congo, until one day he began to live the Sermon on the Mount in their midst, and told them he was going to act according to all its precepts. Before the day was over they had taken him at his word, and the last stick of his furniture was gone. But before the next sun went down they had felt that they, too, must live according to the Sermon, and they brought back his furniture with compound interest. Before many months were passed hundreds of them were saved, and today (1901) the largest congregation on the Congo stands there at Banza Mateke as the monument, not of saying, but of doing the Word of God.

In the last months of the Civil War there was a soldier in Andersonville prison named Frank Smith. The day came for the exchange of prisoners. Six Northern soldiers were to be released for six Confederates, and Frank Smith heard with delight his name read. But a poor fellow with a wife and children came and pleaded so hard that Frank gave up his ticket of release, and let the other be his substitute and go home to the little family that needed him more. The months rolled round, and again there was a release of prisoners, and once more Frank Smith heard his name called and dreamed of home and liberty. But he remembered an infidel whom he had often talked to in the prison, and he said, "I cannot go till I make one more appeal to him to accept Christ." But the infidel laughed him to scorn, and told him that talk was cheap. Then Frank breathed a prayer and made a great resolution. Taking his little ticket of release from his pocket he said, "Take this, and in my place tomorrow walk out into freedom." The infidel started and looked hard at him "What made you do this?" he asked. "The love of Christ," he said. "The Christ that you will not receive." Then the proud heart broke; sobbing and kneeling beside him, he asked forgiveness for his hard heart, and gave himself to the Savior whose love could make such sacrifice possible. "It was not what you said that convinced me," he explained, "but it was what you did."

Once again there came a day when a little company walked forth from that awful dungeon into liberty, and for the third time Frank Smith's name was on the roll. He went to a lad who was dying of consumption. The poor fellow wept bitterly and said: "Oh, Frank, I had hoped that you could be with me at the last. I have nobody else to pray with me or point me to the Savior. How shall I ever die alone?" Again Frank closed his eyes, lifted his heart to God, and formed another big resolution. He gave his ticket of liberty for the third time to someone else, and he went back, and throwing his arms around the dying boy, he said, "I'll not leave you till He comes to take you." And he held the hand of the sinking lad until the gates of light opened, and with blessings on his lips a ransomed soul passed in.

Then on the dark storm clouds of war burst the rainbow of peace. The gates of Andersonville prison swung open forever, and this Christian hero went forth to well-earned liberty with a record of Christian heroism and blessed doing mightier than libraries of books or sermons.

So may we be blessed in our doing.

CHAPTER 4

Practical Love

If you really keep the royal law found in Scripture, "Love your neighbor as yourself," you are doing right. (James 2:8)

Speak and act as those who are going to be judged by the law that gives freedom. (2:12)

We now come to practical love as set forth in this plain, matter-of-fact manual for daily life.

We will call it practical love, for there is another kind of love. No word has been so prominent in song and story all through the history of human life and literature as this old word "love." But the best kind of love is not the most prominent in song and story. There, sitting in that home, is a beautiful girl full of sentimental love, her mother's hope, her father's darling, the idol of her social circle and of herself. She is an example of sentimental love. But there is that old mother, wrinkled and worn by a lifetime of toil for that ungrateful child.

45

That is the love that has sacrificed, suffered and forgotten itself to minister to another's comforts and luxuries. That is practical love.

Standing in that pulpit is a minister who can speak about love in glowing terms. In front is a poor unlettered Christian, who, when they asked about the doctrines of the creed and confession, was unable to answer the questions that were necessary to make him a member of the Church of Christ. They are about to drop him, when he breaks out into a great sob and cries, "I canna' speak for Him, but I could die for Him." Ah, that is love more eloquent than words! It is the love that Jesus talks about, the love that does things for Christ's sake and for our fellow man.

The Royal Law of Love

"If you really keep the royal law, . . . 'Love your neighbor as yourself,' you are doing right. . . . Speak and act as those who are going to be judged by the law that gives freedom" (James 2:8, 12). Undoubtedly it is the law of love that he is thinking about when he speaks of the royal law. It is a royal law because:

1. The Law of the Kingdom

It is the law of the kingdom. It is the one great law that He had laid down, and the Decalogue is but the amplification of two thoughts, " 'Love the Lord your God with all your heart' . . . 'Love your neighbor as yourself.' All the Law and the Prophets hang on these two commandments [which are but one]" (Matthew 22:37–40). Love is therefore the law of the kingdom and the law of the King.

2. The Law by Which the King Lives and Acts

But not only so, it is also the law by which the King Himself lives and acts. It is the royal law because God makes it His own law, and God is not above the law of love. "God is Love" (1 John 4:16), and everything He does is according to the divine law of love. "Carry each other's burdens, and in this way you will fulfill the law of Christ" (Galatians 6:2). This law of Christ is love. The Father's love from eternity reached out beyond Himself in blessing. And from that came this wondrous universe so full of goodness and loving kindness; every object of it proclaiming not only His wisdom and power but His thoughtful kindness and loving regard for the happiness of His creatures. He might have made the earth a dazzling white or a crimson glow and thus blinded you; but He has made it an exquisite green, adjusted to your optical organs. He might have given us food without the sense of taste and without the variety of supply. But He has given us 10,000 sources of gratification through our senses. He made earth a ministering paradise even amid the ruins of the Fall, and fitted us to enjoy it. Everything might have contributed to our pain where now it ministers to our pleasure. "The earth is full of thy riches" (Psalm 104:24, KJV), and "You open your hand/ and satisfy the desires of every living thing" (145:16). Thus we see that love is the law of creation.

But how much more is love the law of the new creation in the gift of His Son! And when He was received back, there came the gift of the Spirit, and all the ministries of His love and grace. Then the love of Jesus Christ Himself, His example of unselfishness, His constant ministry to others, and the love of the Holy Spirit all proclaim to us that God Himself is ruled by His own law of love. Therefore it is the royal law, the law of the kingdom, and should be the gladly accepted law of every child of that kingdom.

3. Supreme above All Laws

It is supreme above all other laws. "The greatest of these is love" (1 Corinthians 13:13). It is royal in the sense that it stands higher than all other laws and qualities. It is the supreme beauty and excellency of all character and being, and the blending of every virtue and grace.

4. The Mightiest and Strongest Power

It is royal because it is the mightiest and strongest power in the universe of God. You talk of the law of gravitation, but nothing draws like love. Nothing lies behind the story of human history like love. It has inspired all the heroism of the battlefield. It is the secret of all that is highest in literature and the story of mankind. It alone can inspire the martyr's sacrifice, the hardships, toils and privations of Christian service, in the mission field, the hospital, the rescue work and the whole story of the service of Christ and our fellow men.

It is a kingly force, the power that moves men. God has incorporated it in the spiritual economy as the force that leads to obedience and every sacrifice and service that honors God and blesses mankind.

5. The Law of Liberty

It is called "the law of liberty." It is a law that is not enforced, but is spontaneous. It is of no value if it is compelled, but you choose it and live up to it because it is your own instinctive nature. You are not compelled to serve Christ and sacrifice for Him. You can be selfish, if you will. But the law of liberty appeals to the best in you, and makes you generous and noble, and brings you the recompense for it in a higher nature and deeper satisfaction.

Yet the reward is not your motive. It is a blessed law of spontaneous love, your second nature, a law of liberty, as God puts it in us by His Holy Spirit and makes it a part of our being. This is the great law of Christ's kingdom, love. Have we understood it, accepted it, adopted it by our own choice, and is it to us now a glorious privilege to be like Him who came "not . . . to be served, but to serve, and to give his life as a ransom for many" (Matthew 20:28)?

The Application of the Law of Love

1. The Social Questions of Life

He applies it to the social questions of life. He shows us that where this law is lived up to it does away with respect of persons. "My brothers," he says, "as believers in our glorious Lord Jesus Christ, don't show favoritism" (James 2:1). There is a blessed application of the great law of divine socialism, not man's socialism, but Christ's love.

> Suppose a man comes into your meeting wearing a gold ring and fine clothes, and a poor man in shabby clothes also comes in. If you show special attention to the man wearing fine clothes and say, "Here's a good seat for you," but say to the poor man, "You stand there" or "Sit on the floor by my feet," have you not discriminated among yourselves and become judges with evil thoughts?
>
> Listen, my dear brothers: Has not God chosen those who are poor in the eyes of the world to be rich in faith and to inherit the kingdom he promised those who love him? But you have insulted the poor. Is it not the rich who are exploiting you? Are they not the ones who are dragging you into court? Are they not the ones who are slandering the noble name of him to whom you belong?
>
> If you really keep the royal law found in Scripture, "Love your neighbor as yourself," you are doing right. But if you show favoritism, you sin and are convicted by the law as lawbreakers. (2:2–9)

These social questions have been practically the same in all ages, and James introduces an element

into human life that has been at war with selfishness, exclusiveness and caste, from the earliest
times.

The caste system of India is the one barrier
against all progress. It shuts away the wretched
lower caste in hopeless isolation, and paralyzes
every hope and ambition, consigning them to
drudgery, and hopelessness. Perhaps the most sor-
rowful feature of the life of India, and the greatest
hindrance to the progress of the gospel of Jesus
Christ, is caste. It is the more aggravated form of a
principle which we find in all lands, and which
sometimes comes into the very Church of Jesus
Christ itself. For example, we have our pew rent
system, which gives the wealthy man the choice of
the more advantageous sitting, and leaves the poor
man to take what is left. The principle is wrong,
and I believe most unscriptural. Another form is
that of uptown and downtown churches. The
home church should be a mission church too, and
all class distinctions forgotten there. The Duke of
Wellington once sat at the communion table,
while a poor man passed the cup for him to drink
first. Wellington said, "No, my friend, after you.
We are all one here."

There is a place for social differences, and they
exist in the nature of things. God does not come
with an iconoclastic hand to sweep away all differences and bring a hopeless socialism. There are
differences. They grow out of successful lives,
they can be maintained with sweetness, and the
door can be left open for ambition to rise to the

highest possibilities. But let there be no harshness.
Let the doors be wide open, and the spirit of love
and sympathy meet from both sides. God recog-
nizes this, and bids us "Give everyone what you
owe him" (Romans 13:7). Impudence and inso-
lence are not part of the gospel of Jesus Christ.
Courtesy and respect to all classes and in all places
are qualities of true Christian humility. But this is
very different from exclusiveness and pride. The
true church should be a mission, too. So in our
family, social and business life, let us carry out
this law of love—proper respect and honor for
all—and yet loving consideration, a spirit of con-
siderateness for those in humbler places, the gra-
ciousness that in every way covers our social
differences by Christ's own law of love.

2. *The Judging of One Another*

He applies the law of love to the judging of one
another harshly, "because judgment without
mercy will be shown to anyone who has not been
merciful. Mercy triumphs over judgment!" (James
2:13). Again, "Brothers, do not slander one another. Anyone who speaks against his brother or
judges him speaks against the law and judges it.
When you judge the law, you are not keeping it,
but sitting in judgment on it" (4:11). The spirit of
criticism, fault finding, and censoriousness are all
condemned by this law of love. Ask God for the
love that "always trusts, always hopes" (1 Corinthians 13:7), and *dares to think the best both of others
and of yourself*. God wants you to look on the

brightest side in your own heart and life and then in others. You will find the one who is harsh and censorious gets the worst of it. Like the scorpion which after stinging others ends by stinging itself to death, that one gets the retribution of a bitter spirit in the misery it brings.

God puts us in the place of trial to give us the opportunity of rising to the spirit of Christian love, just as He placed Christ in the judgment hall in order that He might stand before us as an example of long-suffering love. He lets people hurt and wrong us that we may be more like Him. When God in His providence calls you to these trying conditions, it is that you may have your education completed and enter into the sweetness of the Lord Jesus Christ, and be merciful even as you expect Him to be merciful to you.

The unpardonable sin of the New Testament is that of unforgiveness, "Because judgment without mercy will be shown to anyone who has not been merciful" (James 2:13).

A Christian worker said that he once became satisfied that the worm at the core of much of the work in his field was this petty spirit of faultfinding, this readiness to see wrong. He set his face against it and got his people to set their faces against it by prayer and watching. The result was wonderful in the blessing that had come to the work. The work had grown and prospered since they had put these weeds out of the garden and destroyed the worm at the roots. This curse grows unconsciously. Shall we resolve by God's grace that if we cannot speak well, we will not speak ill of one another?

"Speak and act as those who are going to be judged by the law that gives freedom" (2:12). How do you expect to be judged? Do you suppose God is going to reveal all your sins before the throne, and you stand in shame of that revelation? "Therefore judge nothing before the appointed time; wait till the Lord comes. He will bring to light what is hidden in darkness. . . . At that time each will receive his praise from God" (1 Corinthians 4:5). In that day of final assize, your Judge is going to bring out every hidden motive that could shed a generous light upon your conduct and character. He is going to bring out the praise, and not the blame. We have not been living up to our expectations. Let us ask God not to deal with us as we have dealt with one another. Lord, help us so to act "as those who are going to be judged by the law that gives freedom" (James 2:12).

3. The Question of Practical Beneficence

James applies this royal law of love to the question of practical beneficence, our kindly help to one another. "Suppose a brother or sister is without clothes and daily food. If one of you says to him, 'Go, I wish you well; keep warm and well fed,' but does nothing about his physical needs, what good is it?" (2:15–16). It is doing things to relieve and help the temporal needs of our suffering fellowmen. He came to heal as well as to save, to help the multitudes and to practice His own precepts, as well as to point the way to heaven. Our acts of love and help may be His links in bringing them to see the attraction of His love and to listen to the gospel of His grace. One of the most beautiful kinds of service is the service lost in its own shadow. A saint was told to ask the greatest good he could claim, and as the angel waited, who brought the message, the answer came, "That I may do the largest amount of good without it ever being known." It was granted. It was so ordered that wherever his shadow fell, somebody would be restored, comforted or saved. Thus his shadow always brought blessing. He never saw it; the world never knew it; but God knew it. It was a life of love hidden until the great revealing day.

God wants us to be practical in blessing others. Very quaintly did an old pioneer Methodist preacher answer some friends to whom he had been preaching. "God bless you," they said, "God will surely bless you; God will reward you for this in the resurrection." But the poor preacher did not have much money in his bag, and he had a long way before him, and he thought their love was rather cheap, so he said, "I am much obliged for your good wishes for the resurrection. It will do very nicely for me, but not for my old mare, for she is not going to have a resurrection; don't forget her, if you please, before the resurrection."

4. A Gentle and Peaceful Spirit

Love will manifest itself in a gentle and peaceful spirit. "But the wisdom that comes from heaven is first of all pure; then peace-loving, considerate, submissive, full of mercy and good fruit, impartial and sincere" (3:17). The children of love are peacemakers, and "[p]eacemakers who sow in peace raise a harvest of righteousness" (3:18). Among all "the fruit of the Spirit" there is none more precious than a gentle, meek and quiet disposition. "[T]he unfading beauty of a gentle and quiet spirit" is indeed "of great worth in God's sight" (1 Peter 3:4). Like an oasis in a desert, like a fragrant blossom on the air of spring, like a cool breeze on a sultry day, like a mother's kiss or gentle breast to a tired child, so is the spirit of gentleness in this rude world of strife and sorrow. Good temper, better still, the Christian temper, is the charm of character and the solace of life. It is but another name for practical love.

5. *Expressed in Practical Religion*

Practical love expresses itself in practical religion, for James has already told us that "[r]eligion that God our Father accepts as pure and faultless is this: to look after orphans and widows in their distress and to keep oneself from being polluted by the world" (James 1:27). Practical love can never stop short of the highest of all service, the spiritual help and blessing of our fellow beings. To lead the unsaved to Christ, to restore the backslider, to comfort the broken hearted, to rescue the tempted, "to look after orphans and widows in their distress" (1:27), this is Christian service, this is heavenly love. Beyond your routine of daily duty and your consistent endeavor to carry your religion into common life, are you also doing something definitely for the spiritual help of your fellow creatures? Are you ministering to their souls and bearing their burdens? "I was sick and you looked after me, I was in prison and you came to visit me" (Matthew 25:36). These are His own tests in the great final day of love and discipleship. How much often comes from such simple ministry! The visits of a clergyman to a poor dairyman's daughter led to a little story which became the instrument of God in the conversion of such illustrious lives as William Wilberforce and Thomas Chalmers.

How many lonely women and neglected children crowd the tenement houses of the block on which you live, whom a little thoughtful kindness might find out in their isolation and comfort in their loneliness!

On a stormy New Year's day a loving Christian girl made her way to a widow's home instead of to some grand social function, and, after cheering the heart of the lonely mother, gave her boy an illustrated almanac with a verse for every day in the year. As she left him she said, "Mind, Harry, that you learn your verse every day and that you live it, too." And as the verse for the day was, "Choose you this day whom ye will serve" (Joshua 24:15, KJV), Harry took it as his watchword for the New Year, and promised to serve the Lord. Harry had a roommate called Tom Short who worked in a sugar factory, and after a little sneering and jesting, Tom also promised to learn the verses. The next day when Tom arrived at the shop, his neighbor asked him what was the latest news. "Oh," said Tom, "I cannot tell you the news, but I can tell you the verse." And so Tom repeated it amid a shower of profane jests and scoffs. But one man listened with a different spirit, and when he went home, he repeated to his poor dying wife each day Tom's texts. The second day was, "For the wages of sin is death" (Romans 6:23). All that day and all that night the words rang in her startled ear, until at last she called her husband, and told him she was dying, because the wages of sin was death, and she had lived in sin and knew not how to be saved. But the next night her husband brought her a new text and oh, how eagerly she listened! "The blood of Jesus Christ his Son cleanseth us from all sin" (1 John 1:7, KJV). And all through that night of weakness and sinking agony, again and again she repeated it, until once more she called her husband to her and told him how the past had all come back to her—the teachings of her childhood, the lessons of her Sunday school, the gospel she once heard so often—and with it the peace of forgiveness and joy of salvation, and in that peace and joy she passed from her troubled life into the rest above. All this was the fruit of a little ministry of unselfish love. So let us love and serve our Master and our fellowmen.

CHAPTER 5

The Practical Use of the Tongue

We all stumble in many ways. If anyone is never at fault in what he says, he is a perfect man, able to keep his whole body in check. (James 3:2)

Speech is one of the supreme distinctions between man and the lower animals. The power of expressing thought in articulate language and written speech, and giving it an incarnate body and a tangible immortal life, is one of the high prerogatives of rational beings. Science through the phonograph is putting upon the tablets which will endure through time the very tones of our voice. God is emphasizing the power and importance of the tongue, and it may be that we will find some day that every whisper that ever emanated from our life has been recorded on phonographic plates in yonder sky. We may find that the witnesses of the judgment will be the records that we ourselves have made, and we will realize that by our words we will be justified and by our words we will be condemned, and "I tell you that men will have to give account on the day of judgment for every careless word they have spoken" (Matthew 12:36).

The Apostle James considers it worthwhile to devote a whole chapter to the subject of the tongue and the practical use of our little member of speech.

The Test of Character

James tells us that the control of the tongue is the test of character. A man's conversation is the real test of his character, and a man that "does not keep a tight rein on his tongue, he deceives himself and his religion is worthless" (James 1:26). An unbridled tongue is a sure sign of an unsanctified, undisciplined and perhaps unsaved soul. On the other hand, "If anyone is never at fault in what he says, he is a perfect man, able to keep his whole body in check" (3:2). It is a sign that he is under the government of his conscience, his will and the Holy Spirit. This is a most heart-searching test. Let us take it home. Can we stand it? It was a foolish word, a hasty word, a word of doubt and irritation that lost Moses the Land of Promise. He would have taken it back if he could, but it was recorded. It had gone upon the record, and it had to stand, and for that one little speech Moses lost the hope of a lifetime. While he was taken to heaven, he could not lead Israel into the land which was the type of a victorious life.

When Isaiah was called to his ministry, it was his lips that were first sanctified. The live coal was applied to these members, and the word spoken, "See, this has touched your lips; your guilt is taken away and your sin atoned for" (Isaiah 6:7). His tongue had to be purified before God could use him.

On the day of Pentecost, it was cloven tongues, tongues of fire that came, tongues possessed by the Holy Spirit. If you have received the baptism of the Spirit, your tongue has received the first touch. You will never talk as you used to talk, you will never have the same unlicensed freedom, but your language will be under the control of a watchful spirit. Our words are God's touchstones by which He is showing us to ourselves and to the world.

We find even in common life, that if a man has sense enough to hold his peace, "even a fool is thought wise if he keeps silent" (Proverbs 17:28). Quiet, self-contained people are often taken for more than they really are, while many a man of capacity and many a woman of beautiful qualities wreck their whole lives by an uncontrolled tongue. If it settles our influence and character here, then how much more in the sight of Him who said, "For by your words you will be acquitted, and by your words you will be condemned" (Matthew 12:37).

The Influence and the Poser of the Tongue

The apostle next proceeds to illustrate the tremendous influence and power of the tongue. He uses a number of illustrations. He says "We put bits into the mouths of horses" (James 3:3), because it is their mouths that determine their action. Just as a man's mouth is the test of character, so the horse's mouth is the place to control him. We put bits in their mouths, and by these turn about their whole body, so that a little bit of steel and a little thong of leather will hold a fiery steed, and turn it at the touch of a woman's hand. So the tongue is like a bridle, which can be put upon us. With a fiery horse you put a curb in its bit. The idea is to hurt it, if it pulls against the bit. So God has given to us checks upon our tongue, making it hurt us, if we speak unadvisedly. If you are a spiritual Christian and walking watchfully, you will find that He will curb you tremendously when you speak hastily. If you succeed in speaking unadvisedly, the curb will hurt you so much you will have to go and take it back. He wants it to hurt us so we will not do it again. Don't try to get out of it easily, but let God's discipline be as hard as He pleases, and go honestly and manfully and have it out. Tell the injured person you are sorry, and ask his forgiveness. You will soon cease doing it, if you will be brave enough to let it hurt you. Speak against another, and God will hold you to it sooner or later. You may get over it easily now. But some day when health is gone, your brain weak, your nerves shattered and the grave seems near, the devil will drive you to it by an evil conscience or a sinking life; and you will wish you had gone and made restitution in better days, when God would have made it easy and used it to save and sanctify you and bless all concerned.

Again, James uses the figure of the helm. He says we put rudders in ships, and a very small rudder turns about a very great ship. The tongue is as little as the rudder, but as mighty. It turns round your life and the lives of others. How great the power of a single word spoken at the marriage altar! It changes two lives. A single word spoken in criminal court brings judgment. The single word spoken by the foreman of the jury means death. A single word spoken as a false testimony consigns some poor fellow to an undeserved doom. The single word of a true witness saves a life. A reckless word stops some blessing that might have reached a soul. That slander that you fired, as a hunter would wing a bird in midair, has shot to the heart some messenger of God that could have brought blessing to countless souls, but for your fiery dart. A word has tremendous power for good or for evil.

Again, he speaks of the tongue as the forest fire. "Consider what a great forest is set on fire by a small spark" (3:5). Sometimes a spark will set a whole county on fire, and sweep away homes, factories, towns and scores of lives. So the "tongue also is a fire" and a "world of evil" (3:6). It is an awful figure. If you were to go to a powder magazine, you would find the place guarded for miles around, and within the enclosure matches are not allowed and each party is searched, for the least combustible thing in that world of combustibles would send thousands of lives into eternity and destroy millions of dollars of property. That is what James means here. We are going through a world of combustion. The air is full of destructive elements, and we must keep the fiery darts away.

On the Oriental steamers the passengers are not allowed to carry matches other than the patented safety ones which cannot be lighted without striking them upon the box. A passenger would be fined for carrying an ordinary match. God says "Don't carry anything but safety matches in the world of iniquity." All around is danger and destruction. You can set it off by a hasty word.

Going through the Alps sometimes a whisper will bring down an avalanche, and the guide cautions every one to silence. The air is so sensitive that the least vibration would loosen the rocks and glaciers and hurl destruction on the pathway. So as we go through life let us say, "I will put a muzzle on my mouth/ as long as the wicked are in my presence" (Psalm 39:1). "I was silent and still" (39:2). "I said, 'I will watch my ways/ and keep my tongue from sin'" (39:1). "Let your conversation be always full of grace, seasoned with salt, so that you may know how to answer everyone" (Colossians 4:6).

It's Power for Evil

There is a dark side to the picture. James likens the tongue to poison: "full of deadly poison" (James 3:8). It is the poison of a viper, a subtle poison that contaminates even the good, and mingles with our worship and all our Christian work. "It is a restless evil, full of deadly poison" (3:8).

"All kinds of animals, birds, reptiles and creatures of the sea"—the whole inanimate creation—"are being tamed and have been tamed by man, but no man can tame the tongue" (3:7–8). It is more terrible than the lion; it is more wily than the serpent. It is *incorrigible, and like the carnal mind,* it must be crucified, given up to die; and we must get a new tongue from the Spirit of Pentecost.

Again it is a destructive and consuming element, "a fire." It is a contaminating element, for it contaminates the good as well as works in the bad. If it would only stick to its own livery, if it would only come in the garment of evil and the livery of Satan, we would know how to recognize it. It comes as an angel of light. "With the tongue we praise our Lord and Father, and with it we curse men, who have been made in God's likeness. Out of the same mouth come praise and cursing" (3:9–10). Praying and singing today, swearing, evil-speaking, gossiping tomorrow. "Can both fresh water and salt water flow from the same spring?" (3:11). James tells us the tongue will be used one moment in the service of God and the next in the employ of the wicked one. So it mingles with our best words and works, and coming in the disguise of good defiles and contaminates all our ways. If you want to find the practical side of a wholesome as well as an evil tongue, read the book of Proverbs. It was written by a man who had suffered much from its fiery shafts and subtle wiles, and he tells us there is nothing worse beneath the sky than to be the victim of a bitter and unwholesome tongue. There are four or five kinds of evil tongues.

1. The Foolish Tongue

The foolish tongue, vain and idle. The tongue that talks thoughtlessly, bores you to death and seems never to know its own weakness; a tongue that will go from the house of God and talk all day about worldly follies, and waste God's holy day and your precious life. "Count yourselves dead to sin but alive to God in Christ Jesus" (Romans 6:11). Bring up your tongue and sentence it to death, and then hand it over to die, count it dead, and give it back to God as alive from the dead, and say, "Lord, henceforth my tongue is yours and yours alone." It is to speak only as the Holy Spirit wants to use it. It is to be under guard, and to recognize itself as a soldier that waits for orders. Then you will be watchful in your speech, and all this idle, vapid, empty talk will cease. It is "idle words" that are to be given account of in the day of judgment. Think perhaps that they are being recorded now on heavenly tablets for the day of the great Assize, and ask God to hold your tongue, to so control it that you will be glad to recognize it as the instrument of Christ.

2. The Profane Tongue

How easy it is to speak the words that are irreverent, flippant and profane without meaning to be profane. The worst kind of profanity is that which uses slang, jest and innuendo, other than coarse blasphemy; phrases that have gradually worn smooth like the pebbles, until the edges are taken off, and now seem innocent and harmless, but really are profanity in disguises. These are not the habits of the tongue that is under the control of the Holy Spirit. How easy it is to fall into the light jesting pun on the Scriptures, the criticism of the sermon, forgetting that these idle words may arrest the conviction of your companion, and the impression that may have been made upon some other heart, and so be the turning point of a soul's ruin! All these things will be brought to a sensitive conscience by the Holy Spirit, if you really have yielded your members to God.

3. The False Tongue

Then comes the false tongue, whether it be the deliberate lie, the direct misrepresentation of the truth or the milder form that you call "white," the suppression of truth, the intentional deceiving of another, the innumerable forms of subtle and flattering deceit which men and women use in the business and society of today. You are not obliged to tell everybody about all your business, but if you are reserved, be reserved truthfully. You have the right of silence and the right of speech but whether you recognize the one or the other, let it always be with the guard upon your lips, with the thought upon your heart, "I cannot do this thing and sin against the Lord."

4. The Impure Tongue

Then we have the impure tongue, the unclean tongue, the salacious story, the spicy anecdote that men will tell to each other when ladies are not present, and the innumerable forms of double speech which may be capable of a right or a wrong interpretation, which evil men can use to such unworthy advantage, shielding themselves behind the better sense when they fail to reach the mark of their infamous purpose. Here is where women's empire should be supreme, and where her severest judgment should refuse in any way to sanction it by her toleration. A lady is always justified in refusing the company of any gentleman, if she has to be compromised either by doubtful speech or profane expressions. She will be much more respected and honored, even by the one she is compelled to rebuke, for honoring her Savior, her conscience and her womanhood.

5. *The Malignant Tongue*

The malignant tongue, the unkind tongue is perhaps the worst of all; the tongue of slander, the backbiting tongue, the criticizing tongue, the fault-finding tongue, the sarcastic tongue, the thousand forms of evil speaking, which work such bitterness and misery in our home life, and worst of all in our own heart and character. Men have been driven to the saloon and the pit by unwise tongues and bitter speech and by the lack of a tenderness and love that might have won and saved. There may be provocation, but love can triumph over this.

The worst of all is its dreadful influence on your own heart—the reflex action of unkindness, harshness and the loss of gentleness and victory.

Ask God to save you from an evil tongue, an irreverent tongue, an impure tongue, a foolish tongue, a false tongue and above all a bitter and malignant tongue.

How shall we speak of the malignant fruits of the tongue—the reputation it has ruined, the homes it has blasted, the hearts that it has torn asunder, the desolation and wreck that it has left behind, the servants of God that it has crippled in their work for Him, the wrongs that it has done in time and eternity, too late to recall even when we find our fatal mistake? God give us a wholesome tongue, and send us forth to watch our words and to ask God to "keep the door of our lips."

I have heard of a man cruelly wronged by such a tongue, and called upon by the one who had injured him after the evil had done its cruel work. The poor man, a minister of God, who had been crippled and hindered in a noble work was broken down under the accumulated miseries that had come upon him and his family through slander and misrepresentation. Too late the guilty one found her mistake and came to ask his pardon with bitter tears. "Yes, I will pardon, gladly pardon you. What else can I do as a servant of God? But you will not refuse me two simple requests." And she said, "No, I would do anything to undo my folly." "Take this pillow, then," he said, and wrapped up a pillow in a parcel. "Take it to yonder church tower where we used to worship together, and just open it and scatter the feathers to the winds." She took the pillow, mounted the stairs of the church tower, opened the pillow and scattered the feathers. They went north, south and in every direction. She came back and said, "I did as you asked me, what else?" "Now will you go," he said, "and pick up the feathers and bring them back to me?" "Ah, that is more than I can do. They are gone." "Yes, my friend," replied the man, "they have gone and you cannot take them back. And the words you have spoken have gone and you cannot undo them—the words, the looks, the evil speaking, the misrepresentation, the cruel wrong. You know them now, but you cannot undo them. They are irreparable. They have hurt me, but I am sorry that they will follow you forever."

"The tongue also is a fire, a world of evil among the parts of the body. It corrupts the whole person, sets the whole course of his life on fire, and is itself set on fire by hell" (James 3:6).

The Good Tongue

There are also holy tongues, yielded to the Holy Spirit and under the control of the fire of Pentecost. The good tongue is often a silent tongue. We all talk too much. Hand your tongue over to God; ask Him to take it and help you to remember it is not your own. What will we use our tongue for?

1. For Praise and Prayer

Praise God and pray to God. This will be its eternal employ, the worship of our King. Accustom it to it now. Learn the notes of praise. When it is not praise, let it be prayer, "Lord Jesus, help," or "Lord Jesus, I take You for this." Let it become natural. You can form habits of your tongue. It is natural to the swearer to say his blasphemous word. It has grown upon his tongue. It is part of his physical frame. It has entered into the tissues and nerves. You can learn God's praise so that it will be as natural as breathing.

2. For the Word of Kindness

Then our tongue is for the word of kindness, help and cheer to those around us—the kindly tongue in the home, the business and the social circle. As you go along the path of life, ask God to give you loving messages, not too high or strained "for human nature's daily food." But, to have a tongue always kind, always wise! How blessed is a wholesome tongue! When you come down in the morning, do not forget to say some kindly thing. As you meet people in business or on the street, have a kind and cheering word. Have it for the clerk in your employ, who is toiling hard and wondering if it will be noticed and appreciated. How it will oil the machinery just to speak a little word of encouragement and approval! As you go along the path of life, just lift the little burdens, take the little stumbling blocks out of the way, and scatter kindness as you go.

3. For Witnessing and Seeking to Bless

Finally, the tongue is for witnessing and seeking to bless and save your fellow men—the *consecrated tongue, the tongue that bears the message of God*, the tongue charged with the story of a Savior's love and watching for opportunities to speak "the word that sustains the weary" (Isaiah 50:4). It needs not the lofty pulpit or the learned degree. The simple, heartfelt message of a little child or humble laborer has often been more eloquent than the studied discourse. Meeting at a wayside pump Brainerd Taylor said a single word to a young countryman that led him to become a Christian and a missionary. It was not until years afterward, when the missionary happened to read the life of this saintly man, and saw his portrait on the first page of the volume, that he recognized the man that had led him to Christ.

You have probably heard the story of the little drummer boy, whose simple message led to the conversion of an army surgeon who was a bitter enemy of Christianity and a determined Jew. It is published by the American Tract Society, and the lad is said to have been a member of the Sands' Street Church, Brooklyn, converted in the Sunday school and known as the son of a Christian mother. Terribly wounded on the battlefield, an arm and a leg had to be amputated. But he refused to take either chloroform or brandy, and told the surgeon that he would never break his promise to his mother on any account to taste intoxicating liquor. When the doctor began to saw off the bone, he took the pillow in his mouth, set his teeth, breathed out a low cry of prayer and did not utter a groan. The doctor greatly wondered, and when a few days later the chaplain told him that the lad was dying and wanted to speak to him, he bent over his bed while the boy said, "Doctor, when you were sawing off my leg, I was asking Jesus to convert your soul."

That message the proud Jewish physician never could forget, and it led him at last to Christ. One day in that church in Brooklyn he met the mother unexpectedly at a prayer meeting and heard from her lips the story of her boy's last message, and gladly told her that his prayer had been fulfilled and that his soul was now a star in that little crown. So let us speak for Christ.

Take my lips and let them be
filled with messages for Thee.

CHAPTER 6

Practical Sanctification

Do you think Scripture says without reason that the spirit he caused to live in us envies intensely? But he gives us more grace. That is why Scripture says:
"God opposes the proud
  but gives grace to the humble."
    (James 4:5–6)

Let no one think that because James demands from us the practical outliving of our religion in a very real, matter-of-fact way, that he has no sympathy with the deeper experiences of the Christian life and the emotions of true Christian feeling. On the contrary we will find, as we follow him in his treatment of this subject of sanctification, that he leads us down into the very depths of holy mysticism and the most exquisite touches of divine love. But first he begins at the dark side of the subject and comes to the very root of the matter.

The Carnal Heart or the Old and Sinful Nature
  "What causes fights and quarrels among you?

Don't they come from your desires that battle within you?" (James 4:1). This is the root of all our sorrow and sin, the evil heart. There is no use in trying to put on new garments till you get the old body cleansed. Nor must the cleansing stop at the skin. It must reach the heart and the very marrow of the bones. There is no use in filtering your water with the most improved methods, so long as that old dead horse is up in yonder reservoir. Get him out, and your filtering will be to some purpose. It is no use to apply your medical treatment to mere symptoms, and try invigorating air and good nourishment, so long as that cancer or ulcer is feeding on the vital organs. Get the root of the evil removed, then your hygiene will be of some value. There is no use trying to get the best sort of captain, engineer and crew for that vessel, if the hull is rotten and worm-eaten. You will flounder at sea with the best captain, engineer and crew. You may have the best plan in the world for your building and the best architects, but if your material is poor, it will fall to pieces in your hands, and the ruin will come in spite of all your ingenuity.

So God comes to the deep secret of all our trouble, this fallen nature, this dead heart, the "desires that battle within you" (4:1). What is lust? It is the desire and inclination to sin. It is the wrong love of anything, love perverted, love turned from God to self-gratification. The last of the commandments, that seems to sum up the whole spirit and essence of morality, strikes at this evil heart, "Do not covet" (Romans 7:7). It means you should not desire to do wrong. The principle of all ethics is to reach the will, the choice, the thing in you that desires. You may put a man in a straitjacket and make it impossible for him to do wrong, but if he wants to do wrong, he is as bad as the other man who is free to do it and does it. What God plans is to take away the root principle of an evil heart.

James tells us that this evil desire enters into our very religion, and even our prayers. "When you ask, you do not receive, because you ask with wrong motives, that you may spend what you get on your pleasures" (James 4:3). So the great mass of human religion is a matter of sinful desire. It is just an accommodation to man's sinfulness, another method of gratifying his evil heart. All pagan religions are founded on sin, and their public rites are usually of the most obscene and abominable character. Even a great deal of the religion of nominal Christians is an effort to electroplate and gild their sinful desires. The ministry becomes a profession and an open door for ambition, and the strife of ministers for honor is as selfish and sinful as the competitions of the world for political preeminence. Religion itself is a convenience to keep people out of hell and make them comfortable through a life of self-indulgence here.

But the difficulty is an evil heart. No matter how it is repressed, until it is taken away, sanctification has not even begun. Sanctification deals with the perverted will, the wrong desire, the evil inclination, the old Adam that is stronger than young Melancthon still. Your best efforts will be baffled until you get him crucified.

This Christ provides for. The first thing to do is to surrender yourself to be crucified with Jesus Christ. Sanctification is not improving your habits by culture, nor is it cleansing your heart; but it is handing the natural life over to death as a useless thing, so bad that you can never make it good, and getting instead something entirely new through union with Jesus Christ. Sanctification is receiving Him to dwell within you, to work through you, to be your Substitute, and to give you His Holy Spirit instead of your old heart.

The beginning of sanctification, therefore, is to see that you are utterly wrong in your desires and choices. The very helm of life is wrong. You must surrender, get out of the way, and die. "Offer yourselves to God, as those who have been brought from death to life" (Romans 6:13), and then let your life be all new and divine. "I have been crucified with Christ and I no longer live, but Christ lives in me" (Galatians 2:20). May God help us to see this truth lived out and died out in all our hearts.

The Forbidden World

We must deal with the forbidden world, the evil world, the world which stands for the environment of the natural and self-life.

Not only are you wrong, but you are encompassed with a world that is wrong, and you must get out of the world as well as out of yourself. This is separation which must always accompany sanctification. Sanctification is seeing that you are wrong and handing yourself over to Christ by His Holy Spirit to make you right. Separation is pronouncing the sentence of death on the world as well as on yourself, and entering into a new world—the world of the unseen, the world of the coming kingdom, the world in which God is supreme and you are "hidden with Christ in God" (Colossians 3:3), waiting for the day of manifestation, when your true world will appear in its fullness and glory.

"You adulterous people, don't you know that friendship with the world is hatred toward God? Anyone who chooses to be a friend of the world becomes an enemy of God" (James 4:4). The true reading here should be "You adulteresses." It is not literal adultery James is talking about, but spiritual adultery. It is the adultery of the Bride of the Lamb who is leaving her Husband for the world. She is the wife who is faithless to her Lord by going into the arms of the world. If you are Christ's, you are His alone. He claims you for Himself and He is jealous of any rival. So James is exclusive, that the world must be crucified unto you and you unto the world, just as the old carnal life is recognized and laid over on Christ Jesus.

What is the world? It does not mean that we must cease eating, working and being good citizens. It means that the love of the world must die, and that we must cease to live for and belong to the present age, and become children of the com-

ing age and the kingdom of our Lord and Savior
Jesus Christ which is soon to be revealed.

John tells us all about this forbidden world.
"For everything in the world—the cravings of sinful man, the lust of his eyes and the boasting of
what he has and does—comes not from the Father
but from the world" (1 John 2:16). Here is a trin-
ity over against the Triune God.

1. *"The Cravings of Sinful Man"*

This means the gratification of your senses, appe-
tites, passions; sensual indulgence for its own sake,
whether it is within the law or outside the law; the
desire to enjoy the pleasures of the senses, and the
making of these the aims and motives of your being.

You have to eat to live, but you do not need to
live to eat. It is right to take sustenance, and to
have a reasonable enjoyment in it, for God gave us
our sense of taste. But these are mere circumstances of life and pass quickly away. If they are in
any sense the aim of your being, you are a
worldling. They are to be but accompaniments.
So every appetite and gratification which God in
His beneficence has given is always to be a servant, the handmaid of a higher purpose, and not
the object and aim for which we live.

2. *"The Lust of His Eyes"*

This includes the whole pageant of worldly display whether it be the love of dress, the love of
equipage, the love of palatial furniture, the love of
beauty. When these become controlling, and espe-

cially when centered upon yourself and ministering to your self-conceit and pride, they are the forbidden world. God makes things beautiful, and we can thank Him for them, but we are not to rest in the thing itself, but rise from everything to God, and make all tributary to His glory and lay them in homage on His altar and at His feet.

3. *"The Boasting of What He Has and Does"*

"The boasting of what he has and does" is a higher form of worldliness—pride of family, pride of culture, pride of talent or of any personal quality that leads you to make ambition and success in life objects of idolatry. Perhaps today the most dangerous of all is pride of commercial power, for the men that rule the world today are our commercial kings, and the passion that is hardening men's hearts and demonizing human nature is the love of power that money bestows. It is like the pride of Lucifer, and will bring men into close alliance with him. It was this thing that made Nebuchadnezzar call himself a god and set up his image on the plains of Dura. God is letting it be manifested in these last days.

You can have it in your small world just as much as the multimillionaire in his world. The fire and tinder must both be put out of the way. The world is the tinder. The lust is the fire. God wants to separate us from both by opening up to us His world of love, purity and hope and the coming kingdom where Jesus reigns and is preparing magnificence immeasurably beyond the rich-

est prize that earth can bestow. This will counter-
act the present evil world.

The Antidote

The antidote to the lust of the flesh and the love
of the world is the love of God.

The Holy Spirit that dwells in us loves us jealously. Here, over against the world and its attrac-
tions, God shows us another attraction, a higher
charm that counteracts and counterbalances the
lower. Down through the ages there has come a
golden thread of romance that has given its charm
to everything beautiful in art, poetry, history and
the story of time. That golden thread is just the
old romance of love. Whether it comes down to us
from Helen of Troy, or Penelope waiting for
Ulysses, or the heroines of later times, it is the old,
old story; something in the human heart that will
give up family, fortune and every earthly thing for
the charm of love. If you catch that sacred fire of
truehearted love, and there is always something
beautiful in it that seems to have come from
heaven, it lifts to heroism, sacrifice and nobility of
life such as no other earthly motive can supply.

Now the secret of redemption is just the same
old story of love. Long before the ages that story
began in the heart of God and the love of Christ.
He is the heavenly Bridegroom seeking to win
His poor lost Bride, and raise her to His glory
and His throne. In the 16th chapter of Ezekiel
He gives us the picture of the love that found
her in her blood, and said unto her, "Live!"

(16:6). And then, washing her, arraying her in garments of spotless beauty and adorning her with every precious jewel, He adds, "you became mine" (16:8). Like Eliezer, the servant of Abraham, who went forth to a distant land to find a bride for Abraham's heir, and winning her consent gave to her a splendid trousseau of raiment and precious gems, and then brought her home to her waiting husband, so the Holy Spirit has come forth to call the Bride of Jesus to accept His love and then to prepare her for His coming. His voice throughout the ages is, "Listen, O daughter, consider . . ./ Forget your people and your father's house./ The king is enthralled by your beauty;/ honor him, for he is your lord" (Psalm 45:10–11). The new world of love and hope which awoke in Rebekah's heart gave her strength to forget her father's house and the home of her childhood. Just as today many a gentle maiden, awaking to the new charm of the old attraction, can leave the scenes of her girlhood and the home of her earliest and fondest affections, and go forth to brave the perils of the wilderness, the ocean, the military camp or the toils and hardships of a life of poverty for the sake of one she loves better than all beside; so the love of Christ, when once it takes possession of the soul, is the antidote to selfishness and worldliness, and becomes the master passion of a devoted life. It is to this that the Holy Spirit appeals. His jealous love cannot bear that any inferior claim should absorb our heart or displace the supremacy of Jesus Christ. And so He loves us jealously, and His jealousy burns like a consuming fire.

In connection with the subject of sanctification, it is very interesting to notice that in Paul's treatise on this subject in the seventh chapter of Romans, he represents it under the figure of the marriage union. The believer is represented under the image of a wife unable to obey and please her former husband, and finally slain by him for her disobedience. That old inexorable husband was the law. As she lay bleeding and lifeless at his feet, lo, another passed by, a form of loveliness, gentleness and grace. It was Jesus, the Risen One, and as He passed, He touched her and raised her from the dead, and then took her to His bosom and made her His Bride. And now He says, "So, my brothers, you also died to the law through the body of Christ, that you might belong to another, to him who was raised from the dead, in order that we might bear fruit to God" (Romans 7:4).

Holiness is just the fruit of a marriage to Christ. Just as spontaneously as the offspring comes from the union of two loving lives, just as naturally as the fruit grows from the living vine; so the faith, the holiness, the patience, the good works of the believer, all spring from the love life of the Lord. They are not put on by effort, but they are put forth by vital energy, and prompted by the motive power of life and love. It is to our love that the Holy Spirit appeals. It is by love that He works the work of grace within us. It is the "expulsive power of a new affection" that drives out the world. Just as that selfish girl when her heart is won is willing to give up her little world of indulgence and flattery, and sacrifice luxury, comfort, home, friends and every earthly prospect for the one she loves—suffering for him, toiling for his children and sharing all the hardships of his life with infinite delight, so the love of Christ is the motive power that lifts us above selfishness, ambition and the power of the present age, and makes it a joy to suffer and serve in the interests of so dear a Master, and for the hope of so great a recompense. Would you, therefore, dear friend, know the secret of living above the world and bring forth much fruit? Open your heart to the love of Christ. Yield to the approaches of His wooing and learn to live in His love. So shall your being be filled with the fruits of the Spirit,

> And all your life be lost in love,
> A heaven below, a heaven above.

The Place of Grace

There is the place of grace in the life of holiness.

"He gives us more grace" (James 4:6). That is, the more inexorable His love and jealousy in holding us up to the highest standard, the more abundant is His grace in enabling us to meet it. Grace gives what love demands, and love is always asking more.

Strange as it may seem, Christ needs our love and claims our tenderest devotion. But our dull, cold hearts often feel unable to respond, and we cry, "I am laid low in the dust" (Psalm 119:25). But it is here that grace comes to our relief, and the Holy Spirit undertakes to supply the love on our part as well as to reveal the greater love on His. Do you want a tenderer devotion? Take it from Him by faith through grace. Do you want a moving sense of His love, a joy in prayer, a love for His Word, a delight in His service, an experience of deep and tender joy? "He gives us more grace" (James 4:6). "From the fullness of his grace we have all received one blessing after another" (John 1:16). He does not expect us to produce it from the soil of our old natural heart. It must come from heaven, and His grace is waiting to supply it just as fully as you realize your need and are willing to claim His fullness. Lord, give us grace to take the "more grace" from You.

The Secret of Receiving

How shall we maintain the attitude through which we will be enabled to meet the expectations of His love and to receive the fullest measures of His grace?

1. Submit yourselves to God. Unconditional surrender is the first condition of sanctification—a yielded will, a spirit prostrate at His feet, crying continually, "Lord, what will You have me to do?" This is the condition of all deeper blessing.

2. We must be as positive against evil as we are passive in the hands of God. "Resist the devil, and he will flee from you" (James 4:7). There is danger

that in cultivating the habit of self-renunciation at a certain stage in our spiritual experience, we may lose that willpower which is necessary for strength of character. The true attitude is an everlasting "yes" to God, and an inexorable "no" to evil. For the inevitable experience of the life of holiness is temptation, and the secret of victory is a fearless courage and an inflexible will, quite as much as a victorious faith.

3. We must make a habit of humility. "[He] gives grace to the humble" (4:6). "Humble yourselves before the Lord, and he will lift you up" (4:10). As the valleys receive the fertilizing streams, so it is the lowly heart that claims the more abundant grace of God; and the habit of constantly discounting ourselves is but the reverse side of the faith that always counts upon God.

4. There must be nearness to God, the life of communion, intimacy with our heavenly Father. This is the very essence of the life of holiness. "Come near to God and he will come near to you" (4:8). It is thus we walk with God, until dwelling in His fellowship we catch by intuition His very thought and walk spontaneously in His steppings. So may He "equip you with everything good for doing his will, and may he work in us what is pleasing to him, through Jesus Christ, to whom be glory for ever and ever. Amen" (Hebrews 13:21).

CHAPTER 7

The Practical Hope
of the Lord's Coming

Be patient, then, brothers, until the Lord's com-
ing. See how the farmer waits for the land to yield
its valuable crop and how patient he is for the
autumn and spring rains. You too, be patient and
stand firm, because the Lord's coming is near.
(James 5:7–8)

With pungent, prophetic words, reminding
one of the ancient prophets of Israel, James
has just been pointing out the signs and sins of the
last days, and summoning earth's children of pride
to the tribunal of the coming King.

Now he turns to the suffering disciples of Christ,
and tells them of the remedy for their wrongs, and
the recompense for their sorrow which that blessed
hope holds out to the children of promise. "Be patient, then, brothers, until the Lord's coming. See
how the farmer waits for the land to yield its valuable crop and how patient he is for the autumn and
spring rains. You too, be patient and stand firm, be-

cause the Lord's coming is near" (5:7–8). That blessed hope, the glorious appearing of the Lord Jesus, has many precious applications in the Scriptures, but none is more precious than its application to the practical duties and trials of our common life. It is not only a theme for the theologian to discuss, the poet to sing and the saint to dream of, but it is a weapon for life's warfare—a staff for life's journey, a comfort for life's every trial, something for the housewife amid the poverty of her home, something for the laborer under the scorching sun of the harvest field, something for the workman robbed of his wages and tempted to fight for his rights, something better than our modern socialism, than our Utopian dreams—a living hope for living and dying men, and a practical remedy for all earth's wrongs and sorrow. First, however, let us look with James to the terrible social conditions which he describes, and which well might be copied from some photographic picture of our own times. As we read his graphic sketch of the struggle of human selfishness for gold and pleasure, we can almost imagine the author looking upon one of the scenes in our Stock Exchange, or sitting in the gallery of a modern theater, or watching the carnival of pleasure in some social function or society banquet.

The Spirit of Godless Secularism and Greed of Gain

Now listen, you who say, "Today or tomorrow we will go to this or that city, spend a year there, carry on business and make money." Why, you do not even know what will happen tomorrow. What is your life? You are a mist that appears for a little while and then vanishes. Instead, you ought to say, "If it is the Lord's will, we will live and do this or that." (4:13–15)

This is a picture of modern business in its worst form. The one idea of these people is to get gain and to do business. There is no doubt about the value of money, but we may surely say that the pursuit of money for its own sake is no proper object to any Christian man. As a means to a higher end it is perfectly legitimate to pursue business and acquire wealth; but to make it the end of life is selfish and degrading. But these men are not only intent on getting gain, but utterly regardless of God in their means of seeking it. They form their plans without any recognition of His authority and will. They determine what they will do each day, as if their lives were their own. Instead of saying, "If it is the Lord's will, we will live and do this or that," they ride roughshod over divine providence and remind one of the old farmer in the Savior's parable who had made all his plans and settled all questions in that famous interview with himself, without ever thinking of consulting God, until another form was thrown across this vision and another voice insisted upon taking part in the conference. "But God said." Ah, he had not thought of this. God was not in it, "God was not in all his thoughts," until that dreadful message came, "You fool! This very night your life will be demanded from you" (Luke 12:20).

There are two capital letters which I like to interpose in all my appointments, D.V., or translated into reverent English, "If the Lord will," and I should be afraid to make any program without that little parenthesis. God save us from the worldliness and godlessness of what men call up-to-date business methods. "In all your ways acknowledge him,/ and he will make your paths straight" (Proverbs 3:6).

The Spirit of Greedy Hoarding

> Now listen, you rich people, weep and wail because of the misery that is coming upon you. Your wealth has rotted, and moths have eaten your clothes. Your gold and silver are corroded. Their corrosion will testify against you and eat your flesh like fire. You have hoarded wealth in the last days. (James 5:1–3)

Here we have another picture of our times; namely, the sudden accumulation of enormous fortunes. Here we have not only the millionaires, but the multimillionaires, that have grown up like mushrooms in a night, and who rise like colossal figures by the score all along the vista of our modern commercial life. They are features and signs of the times. They are full of ominous significance. They have "hoarded wealth in the last days" (5:3). They are God's signs of the near approach of the Lord's coming. Half a century ago great fortunes were not unknown, but they had chiefly descended as hereditary legacies from ancient houses. But the colossal fortunes of today have grown up in a single generation. The other day the income of a single merchant was estimated at 40 million dollars. This enormous sum would support 100,000 missionaries for one year [originally written in 1901], and would multiply tenfold the missionary agencies of today and put the gospel within the reach of every human being immediately. What an awful responsibility to have such wealth!

Would to God that the men might be prepared to whom the Master could safely entrust vast resources and possibilities. But alas, the holders of the enormous fortunes are here addressed as men to whom they are of little use. "Your gold and silver are corroded," he says, "and their corrosion will testify against you." Money unused is really wasted, and the possessor owns it only in name. The rust of their unused treasure is a witness against them, and tells how little their trust has been spent for God.

Indeed, poor Lazarus at the rich man's gate is truly richer than Dives in all his luxury. Once, it is said, there came in a dream an awful message to a man of selfish wealth, that at a certain hour the richest man in the town was to die. As the day drew near he was prostrated with nervous spasms and overwhelming terror; he felt sure that it was the knell of his doom. Vainly did the physicians administer their opiates. Sleep fled from his eyelid and peace from his mind, and a great horror hung over him night and day. At last the fatal day and hour drew near. With almost insane solicitude he watched the face of the clock as the fateful moment came, and indeed it seemed as it approached that he must surely die. But at length it passed, and he had not succumbed. Gradually the reaction came and the terror passed, and he said, "Perhaps it was but a dream." But a few days later he learned that at that very hour and moment an old man had passed away, a village beggar, who was known to all as a veritable saint. The old miser began to wonder what it meant. Was it indeed true that he was not the richest man in the village, and that this poor old tramp who did not even own a grave, had passed on to the possession of treasures which he could never own? It all seemed to him a bitter irony. Surely it was.

Thank God for a few of the world's rich ones who have learned that "a man's life does not consist in the abundance of his possessions" (Luke 12:15). The other day one of our greatest capitalists declared that no man ought to die immensely rich, and he is setting the example by the liberal distribution of wealth in his last days.

The Spirit of Luxurious Extravagance and Self-Indulgence

"You have lived on earth in luxury and self-indulgence. You have fattened yourselves in the day of slaughter" (James 5:5).

Here we have a picture which recalls the banquets of Lucullus and Tiberius, in which every costly luxury was brought from every realm for the gluttonous gratification of a Roman reception. But such scenes are not confined to Roman pride or Roman luxury. Our daily journals tell us of social functions and costly banquets held every night in the season where thousands and even tens of thousands of dollars are offered in vainglorious display and sensual pleasure, and the shameful accessories that often accompany these coarse feasts and "bachelor dinners" are suggested but too plainly by the significant language, "You have lived on earth in luxury and self-indulgence" (5:5).

These exhibitions of godless luxury were associated with the fall of ancient Babylon and Rome, and they are, alas, the signs of the closing days of modern civilization. Surely, as we behold them, their dark shadows are fringed with the light of the better dawning.

The Picture of Injustice and Oppression

For the darker shadow of wrong and crime heightens the picture of selfishness and luxury with which the apostle's fearful impeachment of a godless people reaches its climax.

"Look! The wages you failed to pay the workmen who mowed your fields are crying out against you. The cries of the harvesters have reached the ears of the Lord Almighty" (James 5:4). It is not necessary for us to take the side of either capital or labor in the social or political strikes of today, in order to show that this picture of oppression of the poor is not an obsolete one. Go to the sweat shops of our manufacturing cities; see the poor, attenuated women and children that are toiling for a pittance in suffocating workrooms with long hours of half remunerated toil. Read the sickening story, that has sometimes come to us, of struggling girls that have been told to their face that they cannot expect to earn a living merely by honest toil, but must also expect to sell themselves, as well as the labor of their hands, to eke out a sufficient livelihood or help those who are so often dependent upon them. Occasionally the bitter cry of the poor reaches the ears of humanity as well as of the Lord God of Sabaoth, and we get a lurid gleam upon the wrong and sorrow that is done "under the sun," and we say like Solomon,

> Again I looked and saw all the oppression
> that was taking place under the sun:
>
> I saw the tears of the oppressed—
>   and they have no comforter;
> power was on the side of their
>   oppressors—
>   and they have no comforter.
> And I declared that the dead,
>   who had already died,
> are happier than the living,
>   who are still alive. (Ecclesiastes 4:1–2)

The Divine Forbearance

"You have condemned and murdered innocent men, who were not opposing you" (James 5:6). This is undoubtedly a reference to the murder of our Lord Jesus Himself by proud and wicked enemies, of whom these worldly men are but the successors and representatives. The apostle means to suggest to the suffering disciples whose wrongs he has already referred to, that they are but following in the steps of their Master. The patience which they are expected to manifest was first shown by Him who stood amid the shame and suffering of the judgment hall and the cruel cross of Calvary. He exposed His unresisting body to all their murderous cruelty, and bore in silence all the wrong and shame of wicked men. He let Pilate, Herod and the Scribes and Pharisees have their own way. Yes, they might spit in that gentle face and crown with the mocking thorns at will; it was their day, and well they took advantage of that awful liberty, until they had wrought their wicked will to the full. And so still, in the suffering members of that blessed Master the same wicked world has its way. It is a fearful thing to have our liberty and use it without consulting God. You can hoard your wealth if you please; you can enjoy the banquet and the song if you will; you can grind the face of the poor and compel them to toil on your hard terms; you can do all this for a little while, and God will not resist you; you have your way and your little day, but remember that God is bringing you to judgment. The great Assize is coming on, and all the witnesses will meet you face to face some day, and then how you will wish that you could live your life once more.

Do not too hastily judge that God has forgotten to be just, because He gives you such a long reprieve. "When the sentence for a crime is not quickly carried out, the hearts of the people are filled with schemes to do wrong" (Ecclesiastes 8:11).

Human Patience

The divine forbearance is to be our example, and we are to meet the wrongs of men with the same patience and gentleness. Yes, there is wrong. The hire of the laborer is kept back. The hours are hard and long, the compensation insufficient, the whole system harsh and selfish to the core, but it is not harder than Gethsemane. It is not more shameful or painful than the judgment hall and the cruel cross He bore for you. You are but following in His footsteps; you are but filling up that which is behind of the sufferings of Christ. Do not go and fight your battle; do not get up a strike or a political party. Leave your vindication to Him; "be patient . . . until the Lord's coming" (James 5:7).

The Great Incentive

The coming of the Lord is a great incentive to our patience under suffering and wrong. What a practical aspect this blessed hope assumes in this message! How it comes down to the level of our common life, and sheds its light of hope upon our earthly toil! How it goes with us to the factory and the harvest field and sets to music the task of the toiler! That day will bring us the righting of our wrongs. That day will pay us the long deferred hire. That day will put us in our right place and displace the sons of pride, who have so long trampled on the rights of others. That day will make up for toil and bitter loss. That day will put us in the place for which our talents and merits have fitted us, and from which others have excluded us so long. That day will bring the punishment of our oppressors so terribly that our compassion could wish and plead for mercy. That day will confer upon us, if we are true, rewards so precious and so priceless that we will remember our misery only as a vanished dream. "Be patient, then, brothers, until the Lord's coming" (5:7).

But not only is this hope presented as the remedy and recompense for wrong and suffering, but as a great motive in all the trials and duties of our Christian life. Especially is it suggested as the goal of Christian work, and the harvest time of all our seed sowing. "See how the farmer waits for the land to yield its valuable crop and how patient he is" (5:7).

The suggestion here is for our Christian work and our Christian faith. We must not expect the answer and the fruition too soon. The seed must have time to germinate, the rains must water, both the early and the late rain. Many a waiting day must pass before we shall see "the full corn in the ear" (Mark 4:28, KJV), and for this we must look away even unto the coming of the Lord. Not always shall we see the results of our labors in the present life. Like Solomon's temple builders we are but gathering materials for the great edifice, timbers from Lebanon, stones from the quarry, jewels and gold from the mine. But the workers in Lebanon did not see the timbers placed in Jerusalem immediately; other hands bore them to Joppa and Jerusalem, other workmen mounted them to their appointed place. The temple that we are building will not appear in its complete glory until He shall come. Our work is fragmentary, not final. Many a prayer that we breathe upon the air shall meet us at His coming. Many a message that seemed to fall in vain shall come back to us in some ransomed soul in that glad day. Many a plan which we left half completed on earth shall appear then like the rainbow about the throne, a finished circle. That is the crowning day; that is the time of the great reward. Then shall the sacrifices made for Him come back with their hundredfold. Then shall the victor receive the unfading crown. Then shall they that "lead many to righteousness, [shine] like the stars for ever and ever" (Daniel 12:3).

Then let us fix our goal on the heights of the advent hope. Let the point of view of every prayer and plan, every sacrifice and service, every enterprise and investment be "until the Lord's coming" (James 5:7). Yes, and if even much still remains unanswered and unfinished here, remember that this is but half the circle, and the rest will appear on the other side. He may keep you waiting long, and He may hold back much from your view, but though He tarry, wait for Him, for He will surely come, He will not tarry too long (Habakkuk 2:3).

On one of the battlefields of Pennsylvania a dying lad lay on the ambulance. The surgeon's instruments were ready for the sudden operation that was necessary, but he paused, as he noticed the stupor on the face of the lad, and he said, "No." It was useless and cruel to arouse him for such agony, he could not save his life, let him die in peace. But his comrade said that he must send for his mother. They remonstrated, for they said, "The excitement will but arouse him to feel his agony, but cannot save his life."

But the lad insisted that he must keep his promise both to the mother and to the boy, and they bore him to the hospital, and they soon brought that mother to his side. But they forbade her to speak to him or arouse him to consciousness, and only suffered her to stand in silence and hold his dying hand. But as she stood beside his cot, and gently held that hand, his lips began to move. The eyes were sealed already for their long sleep, but softly he murmured, "Mother," while a gentle light fell upon his face, and a sweet smile wreathed his lips, and he still murmured, "Mother, mother! I knew she would come, I knew that she would come."

And so the waiting Bride of Christ has waited long, and has often been perplexed and seemingly abandoned, and darker days are yet to come, when her enemies will glory in their triumph, but "will not God bring about justice for his chosen ones, who cry out to him day and night? Will he keep putting them off? I tell you, he will see that they get justice, and quickly" (Luke 18:7–8).

Will we write as our watchword and our hope, over against life's darkest trials and hardest toils, the bright inscription and blessed hope, "Until the Lord's coming"?

CHAPTER 8

Practical Prayer

Therefore confess your sins to each other and pray for each other so that you may be healed. The prayer of a righteous man is powerful and effective. (James 5:16)

Practical prayer. This is the kind that James describes: something to lift us up; something that comes down to the level of our everyday life; something that helps us in our business, that heals us in our sickness, that reaches beyond our need to others, and leads us to convert the sinner from the error of his way, and save a soul from death, and hide a multitude of sins.

The Common and Everyday Affairs of Life

First, we must look at the place of prayer in connection with the common and everyday affairs of life.

"If any of you lacks wisdom, he should ask God, who gives generously to all without finding fault, and it will be given to him" (James 1:5). This is the

ministry of prayer in the ordinary affairs of life.
Wisdom just means the ability to do the right thing,
to suit the means to the end in view. And so it has to
deal with all the things that concern our life. The
housewife needs it to make ends meet. The skilled
artisan needs it to give a finer touch to his hand. The
businessman needs it to meet the difficulties and
emergencies of his office, to take advantage of opportunities, to be prudent and farseeing, and make
the best of things as they come in his life. We need it
in our domestic life in the training of our children.
We need it in our spiritual work in rightly handling
God's Word and dealing with the souls that come to
us. And in our whole life we need a superintending
hand, a wisdom greater than our own to suggest the
right thing and to overrule our erring judgment and
cause the best thing to come about, even if we ourselves did not choose it, making all things work together for good.

Surely this is intensely practical. We are to pray
for wisdom. We are to bring to God everything
that comes up in our life, and count nothing too
small for His interest and interposing hand. The
incense which was the type of prayer, was beaten
very small, teaching us that nothing is too small to
mingle with the cloud of prayer that goes from
our closet to the throne of grace, and is presented
by our Savior to His Father for acceptance.

So as we look through the Word of God, we
find that secular matters and everyday interests
are constantly made the turning points of greatest
events. A young farmer looking for his father's

donkeys led to the establishment of the kingdom of Israel. A lad coming up to see his brothers from Bethlehem led to the selection of David as king. In reading the story of Daniel, we find an emergency too hard for him and his companions becoming the occasion through prayer of all his future history. They were in peril because they could not interpret the king's dream. Daniel and his companions prayed for wisdom to make known this dream and thus deliver them, and it was through this incident that all the mighty future of Daniel, affecting the history of two great kingdoms, came about. He simply asked for wisdom, and his prayer was answered; he and his friends were delivered, and the way was opened for the highest possible service.

So we find Ezra on his way back to Palestine suddenly losing his way in the Syrian desert. How did he act? He says, "I proclaimed a fast, so that we might humble ourselves before our God and ask him for a safe journey. . . . I was ashamed to ask the king for soldiers and horsemen to protect us from enemies on the road, because we had told the king, 'The gracious hand of our God is on everyone who looks to him, but his great anger is against all who forsake him' " (Ezra 8:21–22). Nor did he pray in vain. The wisdom was given, the way was made plain, and the pilgrim caravan crossed the desert in safety, and restored the city and temple of the Lord.

So, again, we find David in his first campaign against the Philistines, after he had been crowned,

inquiring of the Lord, "Shall I go and attack the
Philistines? Will you hand them over to me?" (2
Samuel 5:19). Of course such a beginning was fol-
lowed by victory. But a year later the enemy returned. Now naturally we would expect David to
do just as he did before. But that is not the way of
faith. It does not count on experience, but upon
God; and notwithstanding all that God had told
him and done for him hitherto, he returned im-
plicitly to the oracle of prayer, as though he had
never fought a battle before. And happy for him
that he did so, for now the direction is entirely different from the former occasion. "Do not go
straight up," is the divine command, "but circle
around behind them and attack them in front of
the balsam trees. As soon as you hear the sound of
marching in the tops of the balsam trees, move
quickly, because that will mean the LORD has gone
out in front of you to strike the Philistine army"
(5:23–24). So prayer waits upon God and takes the
instructions directly from the throne, even as the
eyes of a servant wait upon the hand of her mis-
tress.

It is said of Jotham that he became mighty because "he walked steadfastly before the LORD" (2
Chronicles 27:6). And the wisest of ancient teach-
ers has told us, "Trust in the LORD with all your
heart/ and lean not on your own understanding;/
in all your ways acknowledge him,/ and he will
make your paths straight" (Proverbs 3:5–6).

I recall an incident in my ministry, a quarter of
a century ago, when struggling with a great debt

upon the house of the Lord which should never have been put there, I begged my people to unite with me in prayer, and promised them that if they would do so sincerely, God would surely remove it. They told me that it was no use to pray about such a debt for it was too big—$65,000. It was all right to pray about things, but this thing was an impossibility, and beyond their power. It was in vain for me to say that those were just the things to pray about, that we did not need a God for the things that were within our power, but for the difficult and impossible tasks. Finally, however, the senior elder of the church very firmly said to me, "My dear pastor, we esteem you very highly, but we do not at all agree with your extreme views about prayer."

Acting from a conscientious impulse, I refused to dedicate the church until the debt should be removed, but consented to preach in it. After a few months I was so strongly called to my present pastorate that I felt reluctantly constrained to leave the scene of so many prayers and labor, and to commit to God the things yet unfinished. A few months after my arrival in New York, a telegram came one Sabbath morning, inviting me to go the next Sabbath and dedicate the old church in the West, adding that the debt had been paid that week, and that the old elder who had so strongly objected to my view of prayer, had answered those prayers himself by giving 50,000 dollars. Of course the response was "Yes." The church was dedicated. The elder's house was my hospitable home for the next 10 days, and when I thanked him for his noble gift, the modest reply that came with many tears, was, "Don't thank me, it was the Lord." It is needless to add that the dear old saint had revised his view about prayer, and had no question now that God could do the hardest things and that there was nothing too difficult for prayer to ask in Jesus' name for the Father's glory.

In Connectionw with Trial

"Is any one of you in trouble? He should pray" (James 5:13). The book of Psalms is the prayer book of the afflicted. There is no form of trial which cannot find its appropriate expression in this sublime and simple liturgy. The experience of David was in accord with his poetry. He had learned to go to God in every dark and trying hour. In that supreme trial, just before his coronation, when he returned to Ziklag to find it burned with fire, and all his loved ones captives in the hands of the enemy, while his truest followers even threatened mutiny, and talked of stoning him, we are told that "David found strength in the LORD" (1 Samuel 30:6). Turning to the oracle of prayer again he sought direction, and soon had the joy not only of recovering all that he had lost, but of seeing his waiting years crowned with triumph, and his throne at last established. Such is the story of all the saints. When Rabshakeh sent his impious challenge to Hezekiah, and Sennacherib's army invested Jerusalem with a hopeless cordon, the good king called Isaiah to his counsels and spread the matter before the Lord. That was all. They just prayed about it, and lo, before another sun had risen that mighty host lay dead beneath the blighting wing of God's angel of judgment.

Even when our troubles are our own fault, and have come to us through folly or disobedience, even then it is not too late to pray. When Jehoshaphat found himself, through his sinful alliance with Amaziah, the wicked king of Israel, without water in a desolate wilderness, and three armies were threatened with destruction, Amaziah, true to the spirit of wicked unbelief, turned from God and cried, "Has the LORD called us three kings together only to hand us over to Moab?" (2 Kings 3:10). It was the despair of the sinner in the dark hour of calamity. But that was just the time when Jehoshaphat thought of God and turned to prayer, and soon through the hand of Elisha the valley was flowing with water, and deliverance and victory came. Even Jonah, when he found himself in the "belly of hell," did not forget to pray, and out of the depths of despair the cry of faith met the hand of deliverance. "When my life was ebbing away,/ I remembered you, LORD,/ and my prayer rose to you,/ to your holy temple./ . . ./ But I, with a song of thanksgiving,/ will sacrifice to you./ What I have vowed I will make good./ Salvation comes from the LORD" (Jonah 2:7–9).

Yes, even the wicked Manasseh, after half a century of bloodshed, when overtaken by just retribution in Babylon, lifted his heart to God even amid his chains, and God heard his prayer, and restored him to his kingdom and his home. "In his distress he sought the favor of the Lord his God and humbled himself greatly before the God of his fathers. And when he prayed to him, the Lord was moved by his entreaty and listened to his plea; so he brought him back to Jerusalem and to his kingdom. Then Manasseh knew that the Lord is God" (2 Chronicles 33:12–13).

And so the promise remains for all the tried ones, "Call upon me in the day of trouble;/ I will deliver you, and you will honor me" (Psalm 50:15). "Is any one of you in trouble? He should pray" (James 5:13). Is this what we are doing, beloved? Are we meeting God in our trials, or are we running to every expedient that our own minds suggest, and coming to Him only when every other resource has failed? How true to our experience is the reproof of God to Israel, "This is what the Sovereign Lord, the Holy One of Israel, says:/ 'In repentance and rest is your salvation,/ in quietness and trust is your strength,/ but you would have none of it' " (Isaiah 30:15). Instead of trusting Him to work for them, they resolved to make alliance with the world, and borrow the swift horses of Egypt. "You said, 'No, we will flee on horses.'/ Therefore you will flee!/ You said, 'We will ride off on swift horses.'/ Therefore your pursuers will be swift!/ . . . Yet the Lord longs to be gracious to you;/ . . . Blessed are all who wait for him!" (30:16, 18). Alas, how often have we delayed our blessing until we were through with all our earthly expedients and had learned to look to

God alone! "Is any one of you in trouble? He should pray" (James 5:13).

In Connection With Joy and Blessing

"Is anyone happy? Let him sing songs of praise" (5:13). This is not so much prayer as praise, but praise is the better half of prayer. It is the amen of faith. It is the echo of confidence. It is the clinching of the nail that prayer has driven. It is prayer overflowing into praise. After Paul and Silas had prayed in the dungeon of Philippi, they just had to praise. And so all true prayer becomes praise, when it reaches its fullness.

The book of Psalms is much more a book of praise than of prayer, and it may well put to shame the unbelieving grumbling devotion of the modern saint. If we would praise more, we should have more to praise for.

In Sickness

"Is any one of you sick? He should call the elders of the church to pray over him and anoint him with oil in the name of the Lord. And the prayer offered in faith will make the sick person well; the Lord will raise him up. If he has sinned, he will be forgiven" (5:14–15).

The careful reader will not fail to note the distinction between affliction and sickness. In affliction we are to pray, but it may be for grace to endure the affliction quite as much as deliverance from it. But in the case of sickness prayer is described as a definite remedy, and we are commanded to claim positive deliverance. The promise is, "The Lord will raise him up" (5:15). This is very remarkable, and should not be overlooked. It seems to imply that disease is a special hindrance of the adversary from which we should claim the Lord's protection. This is not only the prayer of the sufferer, but united prayer, and, of course, the prayer of faith.

Prayer and healing for the sick is no new teaching of James. Way back in the Old Testament we find Abraham praying for Abimelech, and Abimelech was healed. We find Moses interceding for Miriam, and her leprosy was taken away. We find David telling of God who healed all his diseases, and redeemed his life from destruction. We find Job receiving the healing touch of Jehovah's hand, and Elihu unfolding the principles of the New Testament with reference to God's healing love and power. We find Hezekiah receiving back even his forfeited life, when he prayed to God in the darkest hour of his existence. And we find the life of Jesus crowded with answers to the helpless cries of those who came to Him for healing.

Beloved, are you thus walking in the footsteps of the flock? Are you looking to God first in the hour of sickness and pain? Are you honoring Him with your trust, and making even the attacks of the enemy an occasion for victory and glory to His name? "Is any sick? let him pray."

For Others and the Work of God

Next we see the importance of the ministry of prayer for others and for the work of God.

"The effectual fervent prayer of a righteous man availeth much" (James 5:16, KJV). And then he tells us of the prayer of Elijah, and the sinner converted from the error of his way, so that a soul is saved from death, and a veil is cast over a multitude of sins. This is the highest ministry of prayer, not for ourselves, but for others and for God. But such prayer is no idle play. The apostle calls it the "effectual fervent prayer." Rotherham translates it "the supplication of a righteous man availeth much, working inwardly." The idea is that of intense energy, a paroxysm of internal force working out corresponding results. The illustration is Elijah on Mount Carmel. The vivid description of the sacred narrative presents us the picture of the prophet on his face with his head between his knees. It is a picture of strenuous inward conflict. Every nerve and muscle is intensely wrought to the highest strain. A mighty struggle is going on within. He is getting hold of God for something stupendous; and, lo, in a little while we see that inward conflict reproduced in the outer world, in the swift hurricane, the gleaming lightning, the reverberating thunder, the terrors of the tempest. This is but the outcome of the forces that had been working within, and that had touched the springs of omnipotence and let loose the powers of heaven. The literal translation of the passage about Elijah is "Elijah prayed a prayer." He did not pray a phrase or a form, or a paragraph, but a prayer. It was a living force. It had momentum in it. It was like the sure projectile that speeds from that piece of artillery. It reached somewhere. It accomplished something.

You have heard of the Boer hunter who went out with an American sportsman to shoot antelope. The American took his belt full of cartridges. The Boer took just one. "Why," said the other, "don't you intend to take some cartridges?" "Oh," said he, "I have taken my cartridge." "Yes, but," replied the other, "don't you want more?" "Oh no," said he. "I just want one antelope." The Boer meant that he expected to hit his target the first shot, and saw no use in wasting ammunition. The American probably expected one antelope too, but a score of spent shots. This is not a bad illustration of the different kinds of prayer. Most of our petitions go up like soap bubbles, vanishing as we gaze. True prayer is pointed, real and expects to reach the ear of God, and bring the answer from above every time. There is no higher service for the Master than to stand in such holy priesthood, and bear the burdens of other souls and the kingdom of our Lord.

"I am one of 11 children," said an old lady. "My brothers and sisters were all smarter and stronger than I. I am a poor shrunken cripple. I have no talent or influence. But I know how to pray, and God has let them all die; and it seems as though He needed me more than all." This old lady used to lie upon her bed and have her attendant read the letters of friends, or the newspapers of the day, while she would stop between sentences, and take hold of God for each need, waiting until she had claimed the answer and recorded it in the Lord's book of remembrance. Need we doubt that the answer came? These are the forces that are making the history of eternity. God help us to be among them.

Lord, teach us to pray!